THE CLASH

Omnibus Press
London/New York/Sydney/Cologne

© Copyright 1983 Omnibus Press
(A division of Book Sales Limited)
Book designed by Alison Fenton
Picture research by Valerie Boyd
Typeset by Futurafoto
Printed in England by J.B. Offset Printers
(Marks Tey) Limited, Marks Tey

ISBN 0.7119.0288.7
Order No. OP 42613

Exclusive distributors:
Book Sales Limited
78 Newman Street, London W1P 3LA. UK
Music Sales Corporation
24 East 22nd Street, New York, NY10010, USA
Omnibus Press
GPO Box 3304, Sydney, NSW 2001. Australia

To the Music Trade Only:
Music Sales Limited
78 Newman Street, London W1P 3LA. UK
Music Sales Corporation
24 East 22nd Street, New York, NY10010, USA

Photographs by Adrian Boot, CBS, Caroline Coon,
London Features International, Terry Lotts,
Sheila Rock, Red Saunders, Kate Simon, Paul Slattery,
Pennie Smith, Ray Stevenson.

Cover photography by Andre Csillag

WESTWAY SOUND

"I think people ought to know that we're anti-fascist, we're anti-violence, we're anti-racist and we're pro-creative. We're against ignorance."
Joe Strummer

"We urge people to learn fast."
Mick Jones

11pm all the pubs shut, the radio reads you 'A Book At Bedtime'. Midnight, and the TV channels have all closed down, outside the buses and trains have stopped running. Anyone on the streets after midnight stands a good chance of being stopped by the police.

It's so grey in London Town with a Panda car crawling around,

Here it comes, eleven o'clock, where can we go now?
('Remote Control', The Clash)

Take a huge city, bombed every night for two years by German aircraft until great gaps were missing from the rows of houses as if giant teeth had been pulled. Thirty years later many of the bomb sites are still there, rubble filled and weeded over, indistinguishable from the new ones created by abandoned slum clearance schemes, all surrounded by huge hoardings advertising cigarettes and beer and holidays in the sun. Sentinel-like among the remains of terraces stand great tower blocks erected in a hurry to meet the massive housing demand. Concrete cells each containing a family and a television, looking out over a desolate wasteland of railway tracks, freight yards and motorways. And living at home with their parents are the Clockwork Orange generation of punks – children of the late fifties, early sixties . . .

"I ain't never lived under five floors. I ain't never lived on the ground."
Mick Jones

When he wrote the Clash anthem 'London's Burning With Boredom' he was still living with his grandmother on the 18th floor of a tower block overlooking The Westway, the main west-bound motorway out of London.

"Our speed is The Westway speed."
Mick Jones

"The speed of a car going down The Westway."
Joe Strummer

The punk bands played fast and vicious. No messing about.

Live at home till you get married and can get on the council list for your own little box in a high rise. London has 35,000 people squatting in empty buildings – no rent but appalling conditions. Flats are impossible to get so kids who leave home or get kicked out usually finish up living in a squat. This is where most of the punk bands came from. Both The Sex Pistols and The Clash had their origins in squats: The Pistols from one in Hampstead and The Clash from West London squats in Shepherds Bush and Queensway. You can just about live on the dole if there's no rent to pay.

The way out for working class kids in England has usually been through football or rock 'n' roll and a good way into rock 'n' roll is through an art school where you get paid a government grant for three years to get your act together. There is a fine tradition of art school rock 'n' rollers: Eric Clapton, Jeff Beck, Charlie Watts, John Lennon . . .

Three of The Clash went to art school. Mick Jones studied at Hammersmith College:

"I was down to, like, just showing up on grant day. But I hung on till my final year . . . I only went to art school to join a group anyway. I thought, Pete Townshend, Ray Davies, Keith Richard – they all went to art school so if I can go to art school I will . . . and meet hundreds of musicians.

"Art school is a waste of time. They can only teach you what to see, not what to say. We were supposed to pick the teachers' brains, but it was like picking through rubbish."

Joe Strummer went to Central School of Art and Design:

"I thought that it was great that I got a place – until I'd been there about a week."

Paul Simonon managed to get a scholarship to the exclusive fee-paying Byam Shaw School:

"It's great because everybody there is rich. You can walk around the college, nick their paints, nick their canvases and they don't really miss it because they can buy some more . . . You don't get many working class kids like me and Mick going to art school. Better than going in the factory.

"I used to draw blocks of flats and car dumps."

By the mid-seventies rock 'n' roll was in a bad way. Most of the sixties groups had become fat and content, their days of rebellion long over. The kids of the seventies could find very little to relate to and the mythical stories of quarter million dollar annual cocaine bills for some supergroups didn't exactly endear these groups to the young punks trying to put a band together out of dole money.

"We have to fight the entire super band system. Groups like the Stones are revolting. They have nothing to offer the kids anymore..."
Johnny Rotten

No Elvis, Beatles or Rolling Stones in 1977...
('1977', The Clash)

Joe Strummer used to go on stage with 'Hate & War' stencilled on his boiler suit, not just because it was the opposite of the hippies' 'Love & Peace' dictum but because it was an honest statement of what he saw around him in Britain: murders and bombings in Northern Ireland and the left battling it out with a burgeoning right wing on the streets of London.

"Things will get tough. I mean a fascist government. But people won't notice like you won't notice your hair is longer on Monday than Sunday.
"What I'm aimed against is all that racist, fascist, racialist, patriotism type of fanaticism..."

Joe Strummer

Black people got a lot of problems
But they don't mind throwing a brick
But white men go to school

Where they teach you how to be thick
So everybody does what they're told to
And everybody eats supermarket soul food.
('White Riot', The Clash)

All the power is in the hands
Of people rich enough to buy it
While we walk the streets
Too chicken to even try it.
('White Riot', The Clash)

"There's so much corruption – councils, governments, industry. Everywhere. It's got to be flushed out. Just because it's been going on for a long time doesn't mean that it shouldn't be stopped. It doesn't mean that it isn't time to change. This is what I'm about, and I'm in The Clash, so, of course, that's what The Clash is about.
"We ain't no urban guerrilla outfit. Our gunpower is strictly limited. All we want to achieve is an atmosphere where things can happen. We want to keep the spirit of the free world. We want to keep OUT that safe, soapy, slush that comes out of the radio.
"People have this picture of us marching down the street with machine guns. We're not interested in that, because we haven't got any. All we've got is a few guitars, amps and drums. That's our weaponry."

I have the will to survive
I cheat if I can't win
If someone locks me out, I kick my way in.
('Hate & War', The Clash)

PUNKS ON PARADE

"What we want to achieve is an atmosphere where an idea can grow and be passed around. It's a question, I suppose, of spirit and how people feel."

At the end of 1976 the sensational newspapers suddenly discovered the punks living in their midst and had a field day with horror stories of kids with safety pins stuck through their cheeks, torn T-shirts with swastikas or pornographic quotes on them, the S&M clothing, the bondage pants, the tacky fishnet stockings and the spiky dyed hair. It might have looked like a fashion parade but behind the torn clothing there was a community of desperation. The kids had wised up and the way they saw it, society was offering them nothing at all. The Sex Pistols sang 'No future'. Many of them got heavily into drugs particularly speed. Their music expressed it. The status symbols offered to them by the media meant nothing:

I don't wanna hear about what the rich are doing
I don't wanna go to where, where the rich are going
They think they're so clever they think they're so right
But the truth is only known by gutter snipes.
('Garageland', The Clash)

No longer in awe of virtuoso musicianship they picked up instruments and played. It didn't matter a damn if you knew which note was which, the most important thing was the energy and the experience of being in a group. It either worked or not. Lineups were shifted around until people felt happy with each other. Mick Jones described the feeling.:

"We went down to Portobello Road once and there was this stall that used to sell old leather jackets, and it used to be very expensive: like ten or twenty quid. Then they had a pile of, like, 50p leather jackets. They were old ladies' car coats in pinks and whites and things. It was before we really had a group but we all went in there – because we'd been drinking and everything – and we picked up these 50 pence coats and we all put them on as we walked down the road. I knew that we was a group – regardless of if the people couldn't play or anything! It just felt so right because we all had the same leather jackets. It made sense. From that day it was a group really.
"In them days it was definitely like more of a movement in terms of people working together with one aim. It's only since the record companies came in that all the competition and bitchiness started. Before, it was like all other art movements, you know, like art movements didn't mind having their photographs taken together and how they all worked together like one group and it was the one group.
"All the people that used to be around were working for one aim – some kind of change really – to do something more interesting and different from what we had at the time. Like, if you wanted to go out there was nothing for us to do . . .
"Up till then I thought everything was the cat's knackers and that every group was great. I used to go to all the concerts all the time and that's all I did. Until, somehow, I stopped believing in it all. I just couldn't face it. I suppose my main influences are Mott The Hoople, The Kinks and the Stones, but I just stopped believing. Now what's out there", he pointed out of the window to the freight yards, "that's my influence!
"I just found out it weren't true. I stopped reading all the music papers 'cause I used to believe every word. If they told me to go out and buy this record and that, then I'd just go out and do it. You know, save up me paper round and go and buy shit."

Mick Jones comes from Brixton. His father was a taxi driver and Mick lived with his parents until they divorced when he was eight years old. His mother went to live in the USA and his father left home leaving Mick in the care of his grandmother in a tower block overlooking The Westway.

He put his first group together in 1975. He and Tony James called themselves The London SS and played early Stones, New York Dolls and Mott The Hoople numbers. They were joined by Brian James on guitar and began to seriously audition for a drummer. Among those they tried were Terry Chimes who they turned down, and Nicky 'Topper' Headon who turned them down. Both Headon and Chimes would later drum for The Clash.

Brian James left to start The Damned together with Rat Scabies who was another of the drummers that they had rejected for The London SS. With Brian gone, Mick and Tony decided to call it a day. Tony formed Chelsea and later got together with Billy Idol to form Generation X.

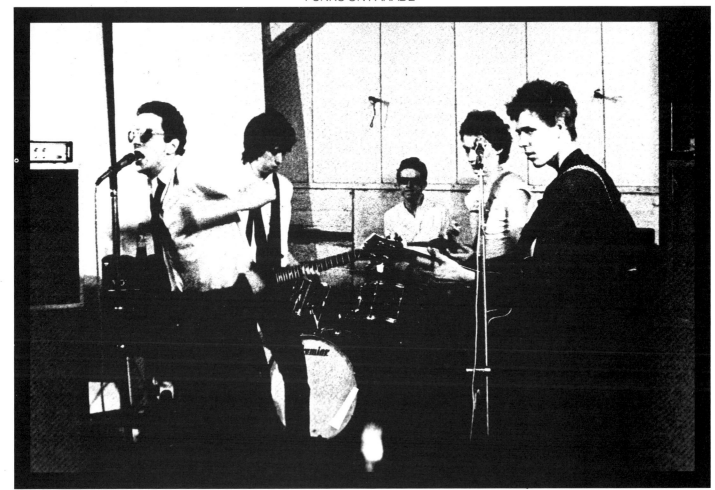

The London SS never played a live gig but had been in rehearsal for a number of months under the loose tutelage of Bernie Rhodes – Malcom McLaren's assistant. Just before the band broke up Mick Jones met Paul Simonon who was to become The Clash's bass player.

Mick asked Paul to join his group. Paul was also born in Brixton. His parents had split up and he lived mostly with his father.

"I had a paper round at six in the morning. Then I'd go home and make me dad his break-fast. Then I'd fuck off to school. Then I'd come back and cook me dad his dinner and do another paper round after school and then I'd cook me dad's tea ..."

He got a council scholarship to the Byan Shaw art school but he was more interested in music even though he hadn't heard much when Mick invited him to come and rehearse.

"The first live rock 'n' roll I can remember seeing was The Sex Pistols. All I listened to before then was ska and bluebeat down at the Streatham Locarno.

"But when I went to this rehearsal, as soon as I got there Mick said, 'You can sing, can't you?' And they got me singing. But I couldn't get into it. They were into The New York Dolls and they all had very long hair so it only lasted a couple of days."

Paul Simonon

Only ten days later The London SS folded. Mick cut his hair and Paul Simonon somehow managed to 'find' a bass guitar.

"I always wanted to be a guitarist, not a bass player, but because I couldn't play nothing – I just used to leap about with it and not hit any right notes so – in the end I thought 'I'll be the bass player – but I'll be the best bass player'."

Paul and Mick and a variety of shifting lineups became The Weak Heartdrops, The Phones, The Mirrors, The Outsiders and The Psychotic Negatives.

"Before we got Bernie there was always some kind of agent bloke saying someone has to go. Sometimes it would be me. I'd have to go! You know what I mean? I'd look around and all of a sudden I'm not in the group anymore – kicked out by your best mates at the time.

"It was a very drifting situation regards who was supposed to be getting the group together. Sometimes people fitted the bill because they looked right like and they couldn't play – they couldn't play a note or nothing – they just didn't know nothing about instruments ...

"At one time there was only about two of us who knew how to put a chord together. The rest of them would be just stoned people, just falling all over the drum kit ..."

Mick Jones

Bernie described the process as

"people from diverse situations coming together and all the crap they've picked up all being knocked off by the other people and all the good stuff being brought out by them being in a group. So that you get something which is totally original rather than ... It's a whole which is different to the individuals.

"Paul couldn't play a note when he joined. Originally the way my thinking was, it was out of the question to have someone who couldn't play in the group but it was good that we took people that were so right for the group and made them into that."

Joe Strummer entered the group from a different direction. He was in The 101'ers, a classic London pub circuit rhythm and blues band.

Joe had been playing for some time. He had left London after art college and gone to live in Wales with his girlfriend. There he met a group who had a drummer but no drum kit. Joe happened to have a drum kit that someone had given to him in exchange for a camera. Joe didn't want to be a drummer and so made a deal with the guys and said that they could have the kit provided he became their lead singer. They agreed.

The band was called Flaming Youth but Joe soon changed their name to The Vultures. But things didn't work out in Wales and after only six gigs Joe split back to London where, in May 1974, he started The 101'ers.

The band did well and attracted a cult following on the pub and club circuit. They even cut a single on the Chiswick label called 'Keys To Your Heart' but Joe was still not satisfied.

Mick and Paul first saw The 101'ers playing at the Windsor Castle pub and a few days later ran into Joe in the street. They were just leaving the Social Security office after picking up their dole money when Joe arrived on his bike.

"We just looked at ya ..."
Mick Jones

"You were shittin' yourself, you cunt. You were going, 'God, what are they lookin' at?'"
Paul Simonon

"You were lookin' at me, but you weren't lookin' like that! All three of you had the same expression."
Joe Strummer

Mick and Paul, and Glen Matlock of The Sex Pistols who was with them, had recognised in Joe the 'right' look.

"I don't like your group" said Mick, **"but we think you're great."**

"As soon as I saw these guys," said Joe, **"I knew that that was what a group in my eyes were supposed to look like."**

Almost immediately afterwards The Sex Pistols supported The 101'ers at a gig and convinced Joe of

what was happening. He broke up his group.

"Yesterday I thought I was a crud, then I saw The Sex Pistols and I became a King and decided to move into the future. As soon as I saw them I knew that rhythm and blues was dead, that the future was here somehow. Every other group was riffing through The Black Sabbath catalogue. But hearing the Pistols I knew. I just knew!"

The date was April 1st, 1976.

By this time The Clash had a huge, cold, damp rehearsal studio in the British Rail yards in Camden Town. It became one of the energy centres of the burgeoning punk rock scene. Groups such as The Flowers of Romance rehearsed there. This, together with The London SS, is another legendary London group. It included in its lineup Sid Vicious on vocals (later to join The Sex Pistols), Keith Levine (who was in an early Clash lineup) and Palm Olive and Viv Albertine, both later in The Slits. There was plenty of energy but no money. No pubs or clubs would book punk bands. McLaren and Rhodes used to sit and puzzle how to get The Pistols and Clash gigs. In the end they booked movie houses and other unusual venues themselves in order to get exposure.

Joe joined the band just in time for the first proper rehearsals and played at the first Clash gig which was in Sheffield in June 1976.

EATING YOUR OWN WORDS

On one occasion, November 1976, The Clash returned to their cold loft after putting up posters for a gig at the ICA. They were so hungry and broke that they turned on the one bar of their electric fire and cooked and ate what remained of the flour and water paste they had used to put up the posters.

Inspired by The Sex Pistols and The Clash, groups started up all over Britain. They encouraged their audiences to do it themselves. They had none of the remoteness of the usual rock bands. They talked with the fans afterwards, let dozens of them sleep on the floor of their hotel rooms with the result that the next time they arrived in town there would be ten or so punk bands on the scene. At first there were a few dozen punk bands but as 1977 got under way each industrial town spawned its own punk scene.

The Buzzcocks, Subway Sect, Siouxsie And The Banshees, The Damned, The Stranglers, The Art Attacks, The Nosebleeds, The Deralicts, X Ray Spex, The Users, The Flys, The Sicks, Suburban Studs, The Maniacs, Swell Maps, Chelsea, The Drones, Alternative TV, Raped, XTC, Eater, Slaughter and the Dogs, Penetration, The Vibrators, Squeeze, The Gorillas, The Cortinas, Johnny Moped, Magazine, The Front, The Police, The Lurkers, The Models, The Killjoys, Celia and the Mutations, The Boys, The Exile, The Members, The Pork Dukes, The Dogs, Tractor, Reaction, The Zeros and many many more.

The bands were followed by local fanzines, usually produced on office or school xerox machines in very small editions. 'Sniffin' Glue', edited by Mark P was the first of these and was initially used as a model but soon all kinds of new forms of layout began to appear.

From Scotland came 'Ripped & Torn', from Northern Ireland came 'Alternative Ulster', then a deluge of mags: 'Apathy In Ilford', 'The Sound Of The Westway', 'Chainsaw', 'New Wave', 'White Stuff', 'Skum', 'Trash 77', 'Lazy Sod', '48 Thrills', 'Last Trumpet', 'Terminal Bondage', 'Ghast Up', 'Gun Rubber', 'Situation', '2nd Hand Nuclear Devices', 'Sideburns', 'Strangled', 'Live Wire', 'Jolt', 'Flicks', 'Trick', 'Kid Studd', 'Negative Reaction', 'Shews', 'Teenage Depression', 'Bombsite', 'Pulse', 'Fair Dukes', 'Heat', 'Cells', 'Moron', 'Pulp', 'Zip', 'London's Burning…'

They often took their titles from the names of songs or groups but usually they were more than fanzines –

they contained highly critical record reviews and sharp abbreviated editorials exhorting their readers to start their own magazine or band or both.

Finally, to release singles by these new groups – which most record companies wouldn't touch with a barge-pole initially – a string of small labels started up within a matter of months. Led by Stiff and Chiswick who had been around for a year or so already came Pogo, Rabid, OHMS, Illegal, Beggars Banquet, Zama, Raw, Rather, Step Forward, Power Exchange, Deptford Fun City, Lightning and so on. In the end the large companies realised what was happening and began to flash their cheque books.

The Sex Pistols burned their way through EMI and A&M to finish up on Virgin (Warner Bros in the USA) and The Clash signed to CBS Records in a deal worth £100,000. The critics and many of their fans all cried that they were selling out – Mark P, editor of 'Sniffin' Glue' wrote,

"Punk died the day The Clash signed to CBS"

but in fact £100,000 was not a lot of money because it didn't include tour support and it is easy for a new band to lose sixty or seventy thousand pounds on a British tour and this is what The Clash did. By the time they bought new equipment there was not enough money left to increase their wages and so they remained on £25 a week each just as they were before they signed up.

They went out on The Sex Pistols 'Anarchy' tour at the end of 1976 but the Pistols at that time were so notorious that many of the gigs were cancelled or prohibited by local watch committees. Their hotels were filled with reporters from 'The News Of The World', 'People' and 'Daily Mirror', all watching to see if any atrocities occurred that they could scream about, and so they had to spend much of their time locked in hotel rooms to avoid the press. Joe Strummer described his feelings about the first tour in an interview in 'Melody Maker':

"All that business on the Pistols tour! I hated it. I HATED it. It was the Pistols time. We were in the background. The first few nights were terrible. We were just locked up in the hotel room with the Pistols doing nothing.

"And yet, for me, it was great too. We had the coach and we had hotels and we had something to do – even though they didn't let us do it that often. We did it about eight times. It was good fun. But when I got back to London on Christmas Eve I felt awful. I was really destroyed, because after a few days you get used to eating. We were eating Holiday Inn rubbish but it was two meals a day and that. And when I got off the coach we had no money and it was just awful. I felt twice as hungry as I'd ever felt before.

"I had nowhere to live and I remember walking away from the coach deliberately not putting on my woolly jumper. I walked all the way up Tottenham Court Road and it was really cold but I wanted to get as cold and as miserable as I could.

"Christmas was here and me and Micky Foote, our sound man, had our little bags in our hands and I just felt like the worst thing in the world that the tour had ended. I wanted it to go on and on. The coach had been like home in a way and I didn't want to get off it."

Mick Jones told *'NME'* about the tour:

"I learned that there's no romance in being on the road."

"I learned that there's lots,"

Joe replied.

HERE COMES TOPPER

The Clash still had problems, the worst of which being that they still didn't have a permanent drummer. Terry Chimes who sat in for them on tour and on the album wanted out. Then a wine bottle thrown by someone in the audience smashed, sending shards of flying glass over him and he felt he didn't really need this and quit. He also believed that a police state was imminent and wanted to escape while there was still time. The Clash began to audition drummers.

They auditioned 206 drummers and rejected them all. Number 207 was Nicky 'Topper' Headon, an old friend of theirs who had played briefly with them in the old days. Headon was born in Bromley. His father is a headmaster at a primary school and his mother is a teacher.

"I first played drums when I was thirteen. I was working at the butchers, cleaning up and I saved the money to buy a kit for £30."

After school he worked the Dover ferry and then on the Channel Tunnel before moving to London.

Topper joined the band in April 1977 and was interviewed by *Melody Maker*.

"I can relate to The Clash on a political level. I've been through the unemployment bit. I've been made to take jobs that I didn't want at all.

"I knew Mick Jones from about a year and a half ago. For a week I played with his band, The London SS, when Brian James of The Damned and Tony James of Generation X were in it too. Then I didn't see him for ages until I bumped into him at The Kinks concert at The Rainbow last month. I'd never seen them play but I was really excited as soon as I did. They are incredible. I really wanted to join. They are by far the best band in the country."

The first Clash album was a disappointment to some people because the sound was so muddy. CBS introduced the band to a number of big time producers but the band was not impressed. They accused them all of being drunkards who were more into business than music and didn't feel that any of them would be able to get the kind of sound that the band wanted. Consequently the band used their own sound man, Micky Foote who mixed their sound on the road. Foote had never produced a record before and so it was not surprising that the sound quality on both the first single and the album was very poor. The album was remixed several times but still CBS were not pleased with the results. Despite this the album entered the charts at number 12 and sold over 100,000 copies in the UK alone. Columbia Records, CBS Records US parent company, refused to release the record in the States because in their view the fidelity was so poor that it would not get any FM airplay. The Clash replied by saying that they would not record any more records until they put that one out. Columbia were not very impressed.

The album was recorded in three weekend sessions in mid-winter at the CBS studios at Whitfield Street, London. The band were exhausted by the 'Anarchy' tour and by the violence and chaos which attended the punk scene. Life in a punk band took its toll as Mick Jones described in an interview:

"Two years ago we did the band's first interview. On Janet Street-Porter's 'London Weekend' programme it was, and me, being all young and naïve, I blamed bands taking too many drugs for the great mid-seventies drought in rock. I recall saying it really well. And a year or so later, I found myself doing just as many drugs as them! Y'know, taking drugs as a way of life, to feel good in the morning, to get through the day. And it's still something I'm getting over right now. I was so into speed, I mean, I don't even recall making the first album!"

THE CLASH TOURING COMBO

With their lineup complete, The Clash took off on a headline tour of Britain. With them in the touring bus were The Buzzcocks, Subway Sect and The Slits. It was always group policy to use their shows as a platform for other bands that they admired and who needed exposure. Their mid-77 tour introduced Richard Hell & The Voidoids from NYC and The Lous, a female punk band from France. This tour worked out particularly expensive since the cost of seat replacement is about £20 per seat and Clash audiences tend to smash them up. Just as the art-rock bands of the sixties took rock from the dance halls and placed it, literally, in the concert halls, bands like The Clash took it back into the dance hall again. From this point on they always tried to play only in venues where the seats had been removed from them.

The Clash moved into higher gear. They flew around Europe for a month playing everywhere from Sweden to France, Belfast to Bremen. Their everyday movements became a subject of great interest in the music press and any move that could possibly be interpreted as 'selling out' was jumped upon.

In May 1977 there was a massive punk evening at The Rainbow Theatre, the first big punk gathering in Britain. The Clash headlined, supported by The Jam, The Buzzcocks, The Prefects and Subway Sect. The audience demonstrated their support for The Clash by ripping up two hundred seats and happily throwing them in the air. At Strummer's request they lined them up neatly along the front of the stage. The Rainbow management were unmoved – after all they were old seats and The Clash would have to pay for them all, it was in the contract. The evening was a milestone in the development of the New Wave. The implications of punk were becoming obvious and Neil Spencer voiced a carefully worded plea for caution in a major 'New Musical Express' editorial titled 'Is This What We Ordered?'

The band were also getting a small but growing police record. On May 21st they played St Albans Civic Hall and after the gig they were stopped by the police, taken to the local station, stripped and searched. The police found nothing but when they searched the band's coach they found pillow cases, keys and towels from the Holiday Inn at Seaton Burn near Newcastle where they had played the day before. For this massive

offence Joe and Topper were charged with theft and released on £20 bail each.

The next week Joe was arrested for spraying the band's name on a wall near their rehearsal studio in Camden Town. He was ordered to appear in court on June 3rd, the same day that he was due to appear in court at Morpeth to answer the charges of theft. Despite efforts by Bernard Rhodes to get the Morpeth date changed he was unable to do so.

Joe appeared at Kentish Town magistrates court and was duly fined £5. On June 10th, which was after the Jubilee holiday, Joe and Topper were arrested and taken up to Morpeth where they were kept in police custody all weekend. Joe was then charged with stealing eight pillow cases and a towel worth £60 and was fined £60. Topper was charged with stealing a hotel key and was fined £40. CBS Records only statement was that the charges were 'pretty ludicrous'. The cost to the public of this police action was estimated to be well over £300. It didn't endear the group to the police very much either.

More problems occurred at the 'punk' night of the 14th Bilzen Festival near Liège in Belgium. The organisers totally over-reacted to the stories about punks and punk bands and erected a ten-foot fence between the stage and the audience. Throughout the support bands, which included The Damned and Elvis Costello, the audience were working on digging up the concrete posts that supported the fence. The scene got very heavy with people being crushed against the wire and crazed Belgian security guards running about. Joe's mike stand slipped off stage and into the pit dividing the stage from the audience. He jumped down after it and grabbed the nearest post and wrestled with it, trying to pull it down. Then the security heavies were on him – 'One of them took a swing at me' – and he was thrown back on stage in a hail of empty beer cans from the angry audience. The gig was soon remembered as the Belsen Festival.

In September came an advance warning of the kind of future musical sophistication that might be expected of the group. Lee Perry, the top reggae producer, was so impressed when he heard The Clash version of Junior Murvin's 'Police and Thieves' on their album that he offered to produce a single for them. The number was 'Complete Control', a song about the

problems they were having with their record company but the fans overlooked that little piece of self-indulgence and lapped it up. It was a very powerful performance.

Next came a four-week autumn tour opening in Belfast, a city that most bands avoided if they possibly could. The tour got off to a bad start by the Belfast gig being called off at the last minute because no insurance cover existed on the hall. The band went and talked with the frustrated fans but most of the fans felt let down by the band. A few windows in the Ulster Hall were smashed, five punks were arrested and beer cans were hurled at The Clash's departing vehicle. They released their anger and frustration by playing a superb set in Dublin which quite a few Northern Ireland fans had travelled down for.

PUNK IS DEAD

They finally were able to prove their loyalty to their fans by returning and playing a dynamite gig at Queen's University Student Union in Belfast. This one went off without a hitch, though armed police in Landrovers waited outside.

The end of 1977 was a time of re-evaluation for The Clash. They had been playing for eighteen months and had a fair amount of experience under their belts. They were still true to their ideals, were recognised as the leading punk band, still allowed their fans to sleep on the floor of their hotel rooms if they couldn't get home, but they were also concerned about where to go next. All around them punk bands were breaking up: The Sex Pistols, The Damned. The spirit which had characterised the movement was fast disappearing. Joe and Mick tried to write a new set of songs for the next album and, as a joke, suggested to Bernard Rhodes, their manager, that they should write it in Jamaica:

"I only suggested it for a joke to our manager,"

said Joe in a *'Record Mirror'* interview.

"We wanted to get away for a couple of weeks and we couldn't go to Paris because we know too many girls there and would have got distracted. So I said, 'What about Jamaica?' and he said no. But a week or so later he came in with the plane tickets.

"We went there to get away from everything and wrote the new album but it was a lonely time for me and Mick. We didn't know anybody and you have to go everywhere in taxis, you can't just walk about. Two white blokes, they'd knife you. We couldn't afford taxis all the time. It wasn't until the end we felt relaxed. I'd like to go sometime for about six months."

February 1978 was a bad time for Joe Strummer because he was hospitalised with a bad case of hepatitis that he caught by swallowing a well aimed gob of spit from the audience. It is possible to catch the disease that way and it was another of the attendant dangers of playing for punk audiences who seemed to think they weren't being proper punks if they didn't gob at the performers to show their appreciation. The disgusting habit seems to have started at The Roxy Club and spread from there even as far as CBGBs in New York. Joe talked about it to Rosalind Russell:

"I just thought of all the hours I've stood up there being spat at. It's horrible. When it dries on your shirt it makes it go crusty. And you can't help getting it in your mouth. And then some lands on the fretboard of the guitar and you haven't noticed and slide your hand up there... Now I pick out the kid that's done it and I make an example of him."

He spent eleven days in hospital in Stamford Bridge and after that had to lay off the booze for a further six months.

1978 was the year of 'Give 'Em Enough Rope' and CBS decided that one way to crack the American market would be to have the album produced by Blue Oyster Cult's producer Sandy Pearlman. Pearlman's ideas and those of The Clash were very different. People began to wonder why it was taking so long to record, a question that always seemed to annoy the band in interviews:

"We want to release an album that's ten times better than the first one and then one that's ten times better than that. Like The Jam and The Stranglers were rushed into theirs.

"Because records cost so much we want to make damn sure that every groove on that record has something brilliant in it. If it takes a year to do that, then let it."
Joe Strummer

1978 was also the year of The Clash headlining the huge Anti-Nazi League Carnival in London on April 30th which was organised by Rock Against Racism. RAR had tried to get them to play several times before but it had always failed. Now The Clash lived up to their political pronouncements and gave an energetic, tough performance, marred only by the PA system and ego problems backstage. Mick Jones explained:

"We said we didn't want to top that bill. We just wanted to be part of it. And then backstage there were all these numbers going down with Tom Robinson's management."

GETTING THE BIRD

The Clash continued to antagonise the law. There was a silly incident where Topper and Paul Simonon shot at some racing pigeons from the roof of their rehearsal studios. Someone in a passing train thought that the train was being shot at and armed police arrived on the scene complete with helicopter, treating the incident as a major terrorist attack. They were fined for shooting the valuable pigeons: £30 each as well as having to pay £700 compensation and £40 costs.

A more serious affair occurred in Glasgow. The Clash were the last band to play the Glasgow Apollo, a venue famous for the enthusiasm of its audience and the psychopathic visciousness of its security staff. The scene looked all set for a final confrontation between fans, bands and bouncers. As the set progressed the bouncers dragged more and more kids to the back of the hall and beat them up. At one point they were diving into the audience from the side of the stage, indiscriminately beating up anyone they encountered. The band repeatedly stopped numbers to plead with the bouncers to stop but to no avail.

Strummer, not normally a man to show much emotion, was in tears afterwards at not being able to do anything about the violence. As the band left the hall to get in their cars, a number of fans criticised the band for not doing enough to stop the violence. Strummer was overwhelmed with frustration and threw a lemonade bottle onto the cobbled street in anger. At once a number of uniformed Glasgow police appeared out of the shadows and arrested him. Paul Simonon, who was following right behind him, tried to go to his aid but all he got for his trouble was a bang on the head with a police truncheon and he was arrested as well. After a night in the cells they appeared at the magistrates court:

Clerk of the Court: "Do you understand the charge against you?" (Breach of the peace)

Joe: "Yeah"

Magistrate: "Yeah what?"

Joe: "Yeah sir"

Magistrate: "Just use proper words will you. What is the name of this group?"

Joe: "The Clash"

Magistrate: "How appropriate! £25."

Paul's appearance was a re-run of Joe's except that he was charged with being drunk and disorderly and going to the aid of a prisoner. Despite the former charge being fictitious they decided to plead guilty and get out of there. '£10 and £40'.

Later Joe commented philosophically,

"Apart from all the minor hassles there always seems to be one incident a month. Maybe we invite the trouble, but it's not so much paranoia as trying to stay aware. We're very conscious of the responsibility that's been thrust upon us."

This stuff about fans staying in our hotel rooms and coming backstage is very important – the responsibility is to the fans, not only to keep in touch but also to show that we do care, and I believe that this group cares more than any other in the country.

I don't know any other group that in its soul cares as much as The Clash. Our idea was not live out their fantasies for them but to show them that they could live out their own fantasies. This is obviously very idealistic...

(Mick Jones. Melody Maker. July 1978)

BERNIE ON THE ELBOW LIST

The Clash were managed by Bernie Rhodes, an old mate of Malcolm McLaren, who because he was involved in the original formation of the group, felt that they should go in the direction he dictated. One idea seems to have been to replace Mick Jones with Steve Jones from the now-defunct Sex Pistols but the group weren't having it. There were frequent mix-ups over bookings, with Rhodes arranging gigs which the band couldn't possibly play because they were in the US mixing their second album. Naturally it was the band that the kids criticised, not their management. CBS, also, found it increasingly more difficult to deal with Rhodes and impossible to find out from him what the band wanted rather than what he wanted.

Finally the band acted. They named their new tour the 'Sort It Out' tour, and on October 21st the band's lawyers informed Rhodes that his services were no longer required. Rhodes, who had a contract giving him twenty per cent of all the band's earnings, sued and long protracted legal manoeuvring began.

On the good side, the new album 'Give 'Em Enough Rope' was released to critical acclaim. Originally it was to have taken five weeks at Island Records' Basing Street Studios but it dragged on until the band were absolutely satisfied. Mick Jones claims they spent five days mixing each track to get it right. It was worth the wait. Even Epic Records in the States liked it and released it, albeit with a few changes to the sleeve, including different lettering. With an acceptable US release in their hands they were now ready to tackle America.

U.S. DIARY

A garbled acocunt of the first US Clash Tour by Joe Strummer:

"We meet at the airport and get on a plane to Vancouver. There seems to be quite a lot of us. We got Baker and Johnny Green our backline crew, and Rob and Adrian who are Welsh sound men, Warren 'Gandalf' Sparks lighting engineer, and Barry 'Scratchy' Myers, the famous D.J. then there's the four of us and Caroline Coon to handle the business.

"'Even Aerosmith don't travel with so many people,' says Epic Records. 'Ah yes' we reply, 'but we've gotta do it properly!'

"So seventeen hours later here we are in Vancouver, Canada. No blizzards, no snow, no Mounties – just the customs. They go through everything, confiscating studded belts, armbands, knives, 'cos they can't find any drugs. 'If we'd known it was gonna be like this, we'd have brought some drugs for you' we tell 'em. But they don't smile they just kick us out, knifeless and beltless.

"Anyway, on with the show. We play the Agora Ballroom, which should be called the Agora Cowboy Saloon. Q. 'Are we not men?' Ans. 'No, we are nervous.'

"But the show goes off real good an' we meet Bo Diddley at last. Bo is coming on the tour and the next morning a big shiny Greyhound bus draws up outside the hotel with two Nashville drivers. It's all aboard. First stop, California.

"The bus is real neat with bunks, a pisshole an' a TV video. It's just come off a Waylon Jennings tour. We cross the US border real easy, no search, nothing, then it's non-stop across Oregon.

"About midnight we doss in a faceless motel. I wake up and as I'm searching for some breakfast, Ace Penna our US tour manager tells me, 'Hey, didja know Sid is dead?' I grab him by the throat 'What do you mean' I snarl. Then as it sinks in I don't want no breakfast. Our first morning in America.

"In California the sun is shining weakly. The other people walk about the streets, weakly, in fact everything here is done weakly, except for when the cops get hold of you. We play the Berkeley Community Theatre on the college campus. Our first

mistake, meaning, it ain't our scene. But we play and they dig it, tapping their biology books in time to the tunes.

"Bill Graham, famous hippie promoter, is promoting the show, i.e. making all the money, but he leaves town just before we arrive. Next night, however, we agree to play a benefit for this youth organization who are trying to open up the S.F. scene by promoting cost price rock shows. The show is really great, the hall is really great, the audience is really great but we gotta leave straight after the set to drive the 400 miles to Los Angeles.

"The drive takes all night an' we test out the bunks which are like comfy shelves. We hit L.A. in the morning an' we gotta play the Santa Monica centre the same night. Me an' Mick try to get a look at Hollywood but we collapse instead. Later Mick tells me his hotel bed just kept moving all the time, just like mine, and we work out it is because we were on the bus all night.

"The Santa Monica Civic Centre turns out to be a concrete barn. I only remember the really good shows or the really bad shows, so this one must have been just o.k. 'cos my memory is blank.

"Right after the set they drag in some Epic people, quite a lot of 'em, line 'em up and try to get us to pose with them. I'm fed up with this, so I look at Topper and he reads my thoughts. 'Let's fuck off out of it,' he says almost simultaneously as Mick and Paul say it. So we do, when the Epic people leave they do not speak and they do not look. The air is thick as they file past.

"Again straight after the show we gotta hit the road. A load of fans give us a great send off so we are all in a good mood as we head for Oklahoma City.

"On the bus Bo sits up front slugging Rock 'n' Rye and pouring out anecdotes from his 23 years on the road. The bus has three video tapes – 'Star Wars' (groan), 'King Creole' (hooray), and 'Blood For Dracula'. Topper sits with his feet up showing off his new spurs watching these or playing tricks on Bo with whom he has hit it off real great. Mick and Paul sit up the back plugged into some jumping rockabilly, watching the endless truck stops slide by.

"*Driving to Oklahoma City is like driving from London to Glasgow 10 times. So I get my head down and when I wake up we are in Texas. I know this because Johnny Green and Baker are wearing the biggest cowboy hats I ever seen.*

"*Texas is one of the best places although I can't say why. We are trying to reach Cleveland, Ohio hoping to catch a plane in Oklahoma City. There's plenty of snow, fog and ice at the airport but no planes. The bus has gone to Nashville for repairs so we sit and wait. 24 hours later we finally get to Cleveland flying the roundabout route.*

"*This guy called Larry McIntyre lost both his legs in Vietnam and when he went for a swim one day in the pool near his flat all the other residents banned him from the pool on the grounds that it was too disgusting . . . so we agree to play a show for him, helping his legal costs, but we don't get to meet him, I think because, having forgot his name, I referred to him over the P.A. as 'The guy with no legs.'*

"*Incidentally, to give you some idea of the*

size of the country, we meet some people who had travelled eight hundred miles to see the show.

"*Next stop is Washington D.C. The bus has caught up with us so it's all aboard. On this drive Bo gives up his bunk to his guitar and he sleeps sitting up. So does Mick because nothing on earth will tempt him to get back in one of the bunks.*

"*Meanwhile outside it's 32 below zero and as we are filling up some place the brakes freeze up and are locked solid. So we have to sit and wait a few hours for them to thaw.*

"*Those of you who stayed awake in school will know this is the US capital. Strangely enough most of the population is black, which makes all the white politicians a little nervous. We was gonna pay a call on Jimmy Carter but he was down in Mexico, having a massage. So we played D.C. and headed out for Boston. Even though this was only last week my memory has gone again so let's say it was okay and get on with it, which means New York! New York! (so good they named it twice etc.)*

"New York is definitely an o.k. town. All the streets are straight and it's laid out like a chess board. Some parts are dead flash like Manhattan and some parts are burnt out slums like the South Bronx.

"We was playing the Palladium, a bit like the Rainbow. This was the third gig in three days, and with all the travelling we was pretty knackered. During the sound check I over-heard a Yank talking to his mate 'Wow, these guys have had it, they can hardly stand up, never mind play!'

"Then Bo told me the worst audiences in the US were Detroit and NYC. 'If you can play New York, you can play anywhere.'

"By gig time the place was packed, and all the top liggers in town were there. We were plenty nervous. Half-way through the show I checked the audience and became convinced that we were going down like a ton of bricks. But like they say it's a tough town and by the end of the day we managed to whip it out and give 'em some of our best.

"We stuck around for a day or so to see the sights like studio 54 which is okay but nothing to write home about. To get in without paying you have to turn up with Andy Warhol.

"One more show to go, in Toronto. We fly there to do the gig which is in a cinema. The dressing room actually is a toilet and the P.A. sounds as if it's filled with hamsters on coke. Even though it sounds rough we really enjoy it and so do they, storming the stage at the end English style. One of the funniest things I ever saw was these two bouncers trying to hold the whole audience back. Just the two of them! After the first number they were swamped so they gave up and went home.

"And the next day so did we.

"To break, crack, storm or blitz America you have to work as hard as Elvis Costello, shake hands and smile like The Boomtown Rats, and sound like Dire Straits. Of the three, we could make the first but not the rest so we are going to go back to play the US again but we must also play Britain, Japan, Europe, Australia, and it's fair shares all round. Hey! I hear they're really rocking in Russia . . "

43

PRODUCT FOR COLUMBIA

The Clash needed to go to America to prove to Epic, their record company in the USA, that they could sell records in the States despite sounding rather different from Fleetwood Mac. Epic, however, weren't too helpful, pleading that with two bands already on the road, they didn't think they could afford tour support for a third, but eventually, they agreed to contribute $30,000 towards costs. All the arrangements were made by stand-in manager Caroline Coon, who also lived with Paul Simonon, but even then it was touch and go, as the group only acquired the necessary work permits at the last minute. This could have been an even bigger problem, but the situation was probably eased by the fact that 'Give 'Em Enough Rope' had been voted *'LP Of The Year'* in the influential and ultra-establishment *'Time'* magazine. Calling the trip *'The Pearl Harbour '79 Tour',* the Clash sold out every venue, proving beyond all doubt that America wanted to hear the kind of music that only they could provide. They returned to Britain an improved band.

The members of the group also realised that things were changing, and, in Joe's words, everything had to go back to the drawing board, including their appearance:

"We don't walk around with green hair and bondage trousers anymore. We just want to look, sort of, flash these days."

Which is what the best rock 'n' roll has always been about. Musically speaking, he told Dave McCullough and Garry Bushell where The Clash were at:

"At the moment, we've got a lot of rock 'n' roll power. We're in between the lands of reggae and disco with pick-axes, chopping up the borders. We're really chopping hard, because we've got that rock 'n' roll power to chop with, you know? We're really throwing reggae and disco over our shoulders, because they've both had it . . ."

The American tour had been a great success, and The Clash returned triumphantly to Britain, ready for some hard work. They had been making a film with Jack Hazan and David Mingay, the directors who had previously made a celebrated movie about painter David Hockney, 'A Bigger Splash' – now Hazan and Mingay were making a quasi-documentary featuring The

Clash, plus Ray Gange, an old acquaintance of Joe Strummer's, who had no previous acting experience. Gange deteriorates as the film progresses, eventually losing his job as a roadie with The Clash because he is constantly drunk. In fact, the film, which was originally titled 'Rudi Can't Fail', paralleled the truth, and Gange finally left to live in California after apparently beating up the film directors, but many incidents which had occurred during The Clash's career, including the arrests in Glasgow and the massive Anti-Nazi league rally, are faithfully recorded (or in some cases recreated) on film, together with superb concert footage. On their return from the U.S. tour, the band completed their side of the work on the film, and the directors began the work of editing.

Even though they had recorded more than half an hour's worth of music for the film, The Clash went into rehearsal to prepare to cut some new tracks, the first results of which emerged as the 'Cost Of Living' EP. Despite their continued claims that they were not a political band, the EP was released on election day, and as well as including some brand new recordings, featured a new recording of 'Capital Radio', which had previously been available only through *'New Musical Express'.* Original copies were supposedly fetching £40 so it was a very good idea to provide a better version, and one which could be obtained much more easily and cheaply. The track on the EP which gained most radio play was 'I Fought The Law', and the record reached number twenty-two in the British charts, while in the States, 'I Fought The Law' was released as a normal single. Although it didn't feature in the charts, it did receive a good deal of airplay, which was a breakthrough of sorts. Things were going well again.

By mid-1979, 'Give 'Em Enough Rope' had sold well enough in the USA during ten weeks in the LP chart to make Epic think again about their decision not to release the classic first LP, although 'The Clash' had apparently become one of the biggest selling imports ever. During August 1979, it was finally easily available in America, although four tracks from the English version of the LP were omitted, and replaced by later tracks which had appeared on singles in Britain, but not in America. The LP was a reasonable success, peaking in the LP chart around the 120 mark, just as 'Rope' had. Not that the group had much time to cele-

brate. It was now time for a third album to be recorded, and third albums often turn out to be the most difficult to make. All the original well-established material has been used on the first album, the new ideas occurring as a result of the first flush of success usually make up a good deal of what appears on the second LP, and by the third album, the majority of bands are too exhausted and too busy to be able to write new songs as good as they want or could provide in different circumstances. Fortunately, this didn't apply to The Clash – Mick Jones was developing as a vocalist, and as the early days of punk were receding fast, they decided that not all their repertoire needed to be played at breakneck speed. It even occurred to them that it might be an advantage to perform the songs more slowly in order that people could hear and understand the lyrics.

Joe Strummer: "We thought now is the time to sit down and write a load of new songs and throw all the bollocks out of the window. Forge on new. We went and retreated into Pimlico and we stayed there for a couple of months, writing every day and recording."

Mick Jones: "In Pimlico we were all on our own. It was the only way we could survive."

Jones also explained to Paul Morley in *'New Musical Express'* how he saw punk:

"Punk's now become 'Oh yeah, he's got zips all over him sewed on by his mother and he's shouting in Cockney, making no attempt to sing from the heart and the guitarist is deliberately playing monotonously, and

they're all playing as fast as possible, so this is punk, so yeah, I can dig this!' There are some people who are becoming snobs.

"I don't want to see punk as another slavish attitude and image and everything is pre-planned and pre-thought out for you to slip into comfortably, like, say, Mod is.

"I vote for the weirdo. I vote for the loonies. I vote for the people off the left wall. I vote for the individuals."

Their choice of producer was inspired – Guy Stevens, the legendary sixties pill-head and the moving force behind Island Records' 'great unknowns' label, *Sue*, which released such rock 'n' roll greats as Professor Longhair in this country, and later was responsible for helping Mott the Hoople to emerge. The Clash clicked with Stevens and recorded so much material so quickly that it became obvious that they had a double album – at least – on their hands.

This soon became a problem for the group, as they were well aware that their fans had very little money, but negotiations with CBS eventually provided an excellent compromise: the two records would be packaged in a single sleeve (thereby saving money) and the double album would retail for a fiver. Recording the album only took a month, and then The Clash returned to the States to consolidate the good work they had done there earlier.

**"We're stepping into a few areas that we've left untouched, like sexuality. Things like that: urban psychosis, like plumbing the depths."
Joe Strummer**

BLACKHILL AT THE HELM

The Clash now teamed up with the management team of Peter Jenner and Andrew King of Blackhill, a company originally formed by King and Jenner to manage The Pink Floyd back in the sixties, although by this time the Floyd were long gone. However, Blackhill had a reputation for being able to handle volatile artists – everyone from Syd Barrett to Roy Harper – and so the company was a good choice. Blackhill had also been responsible for the carefully planned rise to fame of Ian Dury, which must have been a major point in their favour, while Blackhill jack-of-all-trades Kosmo Vinyl was also a great supporter of The Clash, and later would become the group's spokesman.

One of the first things Blackhill did on behalf of The Clash was to try to prevent the film (by now titled 'Rude Boy') from being released on the grounds that it por-trayed the band as political – the new Clash image was obviously to be that of a hard rocking apolitical outfit which didn't want its past trailing behind it like an alba-tross. However, although none of The Clash had sign-ed a contract for the film, Mingay and Hazan did have one signed by Bernard Rhodes when he was manag-ing the band, and Joe and Co. had accepted and cashed their wages cheques during the time that the film was being made. At that rate, there wasn't much that could be done, and the film eventually opened during March 1980, at the Prince Charles Theatre in London, although even three years later, no sound-track LP from the film has been released, at least not officially.

'The Clash Take The Fifth' tour of the U.S.A. became literally that, when Mickey Gallagher, organ player with Ian Dury and The Blockheads, joined The Clash in New York and played with them for the rest of the tour, which was extended, due to its success, from six weeks to two months. Gallagher had never seen The Clash play until he was actually on stage with them, which was certainly a case of jumping in at the deep end. It was an interesting idea and even though critics noted that the keyboard player's contributions were minimal, it showed that the group were more than willing to explore new areas – never closed minded, The Clash would use strings if they felt a song genuinely needed them for the best possible outcome.

The tour was an even greater success than before, with most venues selling out, and with the added impetus of radio and press interviews wherever they went, overseen and organised by Kosmo Vinyl. The tour was also a good opportunity for Mick Jones to be reunited with his mother who now lived in America, and who proudly watched her son's group playing in Minneapolis. One event at which The Clash were invited to play, but refused, was the MUSE (Musicians United For Safe Energy) series of concerts at Madison Square Garden in New York, the results of which were released on a triple album with the title 'No Nukes' – some idea of The Clash's standing in America can be gleaned from the fact that among the other star names on the bill were famous early seventies performers like Crosby, Stills & Nash, James Taylor and Carly Simon, as well as Tom Petty and Bruce Springsteen ...

On their return to Britain, The Clash found that 'Rude Boy' was close to completion and that the double LP, 'London Calling', was also due for imminent release. Taking Mickey Gallagher into the studios with them for the first time, they quickly cut several tracks which they produced themselves, the best of which, an update of a reggae song by Willi Williams, 'Armagideon Time', was considered for inclusion on the double LP, but was subsequently released on a single with the LP's title track. This single became the group's biggest hit to date, peaking just outside the Top Ten, and featuring in the charts for more than two months, while the LP did even better, remaining in the LP chart's Top Ten for several weeks at the start of the new decade.

The album was particularly notable for several reasons – the advertising campaign was based around a vintage picture of Elvis Presley, which was partly reflected in the the front sleeve photograph showing Paul Simonon using his bass guitar like an axe, but the main thrust was the music and the sound, which Guy Stevens and engineer Bill Price had contrived to greatly clarify. The group also ventured into neo-rockabilly (via Vince Taylor's 'Brand New Cadillac') and post-war modern jazz ('Jimmy Jazz'), but Joe's "urban psychosis" was strongly expressed in tracks like 'Hateful', 'Rudi Can't Fail', 'Lost In The Supermarket' (sung by Mick Jones) and 'Guns Of Brixton' (written and sung by Paul Simonon). Together with some reggae and several songs with political leanings (like 'Spanish Bombs' and 'Working For The

Clampdown'), and a reworking of the 'Staggerlee' legend titled 'Wrong 'Em Boyo' and a song about Montgomery Clift ('The Right Profile'), 'London Calling' was (and is) a truly inspired album, and as critics noted, found The Clash relaxing on record for the first time, as well as sounding organised. Even news of the forth-coming release of an album by The 101'ers, featuring Joe, failed to deflect record buyers from 'London Calling'. The Christmas, 1979, period also saw the announcement of dates for a long awaited British tour, to be called 'The Sixteen Tons Tour', while the group were one of several big names, headed by Paul McCartney & Wings, plus Queen and Elvis Costello, who appeared in a series of concerts for the starving people of Kampuchea during the final week of the 1970s. The concerts were recorded, and The Clash performed 'Armigideon Time' on the double LP of the concerts released during 1981.

One more milestone which emerged from the 'London Calling' LP was a track which appeared at the end of the fourth and last side of the LP, but was not mentioned either on the album sleeve or the record label, 'Train In Vain'. When it was released in America

as a single, 'Train In Vain' became the group's first Top Thirty hit, and no doubt helped to propel the album into a similar position in the American LP chart.

The first British tour of the new decade by The Clash produced both highlights and low points – a number of gigs found the group sharing the billing with Ian Dury, who was, of course, also managed by Black-hill, while Pete Townshend of The Who joined The Clash onstage at Brighton for several numbers. However, a series of injuries to Topper Headon resulted in several dates having to be postponed, while Topper and Joe were the subjects of a police drug squad raid on a Southsea hotel. Meanwhile, 'Rude Boy' was nominated as the British entry in the Berlin Film Festival, but trouble with the censors was predicted, as the film contained "a very high obscene words count". The group weren't too concerned, of course, especially as they were due for another American tour, while Paul Simonon was probably even less interested, as he had been invited to appear in a film without the rest of the group, 'All Washed Up', a Lou Adler movie to be shot in Vancouver.

THE CLASH CRACK IT

The US tour was even more successful than previous trips, as 'London Calling' was still featuring in the Top Fifty of the LP chart, which helped to ensure that the tour was a sell-out. The Clash were even featured on the cover of the influential *'Rolling Stone'* magazine, often regarded as a barometer of popular musical taste in America, and the response was so great that the group were invited back to the States as soon as they could make it.

During May, 1980, an unfortunate incident occurred at a Clash gig in Hamburg, when an audience of young punks dressed in punk uniforms of 1976, British vintage, turned into a howling, beer-throwing mob, demanding old material from the band. Joe lost his cool and was provoked into clubbing a German punk over the head with his guitar, and was arrested, and only released by the police when it became clear that he wasn't drunk. It was just one of a number of problems which the group in general, and Joe in particular, found themselves grappling with during this unhappy period.

Rumours of this discord within The Clash camp were starting to circulate, and during a visit to America in June, when the band were recording at Electric Ladyland Studios on 8th Street, the recording facility built and paid for by Jimi Hendrix, there was a report of fisticuffs between Joe and Mick over whether The Clash should play one of their early anthems, 'White Riot', during the American tour. Joe apparently won the fight, and the group did play 'White Riot', but Joe was still unhappy, and during July, he told *'New Musical Express'*:

"It's all over, I'm fed up, and I'm building my own recording studio."

Paul was still working on the 'All Washed Up' film, while Mick was working with his new girl friend, Ellen Foley, on her second LP, and took Topper over to America to add some Clash-style drumming to Ellen's record. The friction seemed to be lessening, and it was revealed that the group had aired their views at a meeting held in an aircraft over Iceland! Even curioser was the information that The Clash were featuring in the U.S. Disco chart along with such equally unlikely acts as Gang Of Four, The Cars and The Pretenders. The summer of 1980 saw Joe Strummer also becoming involved in outside record production, when he agreed to produce a single for The Little Roosters, a young English band whose bass player had apparently promoted a couple of gigs for The Clash, and therefore not only knew Joe, but had also gained his trust. While the idea had been to cut four tracks and make the best

two a single, recording went so well that fourteen tracks were completed and mixed in under a week.

During this production stint, Joe talked to Roy Carr of *'New Musical Express'* about the rumours of the band splitting up, which suggested that Joe had decided to give up, if not music, then being a member of The Clash. Referring to the incident in Hamburg, he said:

"I nearly murdered somebody and it made me realise that there must be another way of facing violence... you can't face violence with violence, it just doesn't work. I was emotionally shattered... completely disheartened to see what's happened to the seeds of what we've planted. If those pricks and kids like them are the fruits of our labours, then they're much worse than those people they were meant to replace.

"If I'm going to be pushed into a situation whereby there's even the remotest possibility that I might kill or maim a member of the audience, what on earth is the point of what we're doing? Anyway, I don't believe we've done any good at all. What we've done amounts to nothing."

Nevertheless, Joe returned with the rest of The Clash to Wessex Studios in London for further work on the new LP, which this time was produced by the group themselves, although with engineer Bill Price, who had been so helpful on 'London Calling', at the controls again.

Despite Joe's further quote to Roy Carr,

"As far as business is concerned, I've given up trying to be idealistic",

the new Clash album was shaping up to be even more expansive than 'London Calling', although outside influences were, as ever, hardly facilitating the task of recording. Three members of The Blockheads, who had been appearing on 'Top Of The Pops' dressed up in police uniforms, decided to pay a call on their mates in The Clash, who were still in the recording studio, and their arrival reportedly nearly induced heart failure among certain individuals in The Clash camp, while during October, Joe was busted again by the SPG (Special Patrol Group) under the notorious 'sus' (suspicion) laws. The Clash also decided at this point to terminate their management arrangement with Blackhill, although a boost came with the publication of an excellent book of photographs of the group taken by ace lenslady Pennie Smith, and with some captions supplied by The Clash themselves.

DRIFTING THROUGH '80

While the first half of 1980 had been fairly quiet for the group in terms of new records to follow the success of 'London Calling', the second half of the year saw the release of two more hit singles in Britain. The first one, 'Bank Robber', reached number 12 in the charts, and was produced by the group's reggae star protégé, Mickey Dread, who was himself the featured artist on the B-side of the record with a track titled 'Rockers Galore . . . UK Tour'. The second single from this period, which was the first the general public would hear of the new recordings for the forthcoming album, was 'The Call Up', which was somewhat less successful, perhaps due to a combination of several factors – apart from being released shortly before Christmas, 'The Call Up' soon became available as part of the new album, and was also regarded as somewhat monotonous and also perhaps needlessly political. Its message, to try to end National Service – the address

of the American organisation, 'Immobilise Against The Draft' was printed on the sleeve – may have been of little interest in this country, where National Service had been abolished long before, while the B-side, 'Stop The World', also had an address on the sleeve, this time of the Campaign For Nuclear Disarmament.

The single was even less successful in the U.S.A. when it was released there in April, 1981, but by that time, the Clash fans of America had been cheered by the release of a specially compiled ten inch LP, 'Black Market Clash'. This contained nine tracks, most of which had been unavailable in America except as imports, as many were items released only on the B-sides of British 45s. While it could hardly be expected to equal the performance of the 'London Calling' album, 'Black Market Clash' achieved a respectably high position in the American Top 100 LP chart.

THREE FROM THE REBELS

Then it was time for the new LP to be unveiled – a thirty-six track three LP set, once again in a single sleeve (to keep the price down) titled 'Sandinista'. That title was highly significant, and referred to the Nicaraguan army of freedom fighters known as the Sandinista, who toppled the ruling (and U.S. backed) Somosa regime in a bitter and prolonged struggle which produced many casualties. As the record company biography for The Clash notes, "This did not help the record too much in America," and the initial critical reaction in Britain was hardly any improvement.

It was probably just as well that as the critics were starting to sharpen their poison pens, the respected American magazine, *'Downbeat',* voted The Clash the Top Rock Group in a poll – that, at least, was some small consolation for the accusations dished out in the British music weeklies by the band's one time fans, although the opportunity to wax poetic was accepted gladly by writers who had previously felt The Clash were beyond reproach. In *'Record Mirror',* John Shearlaw wrote,'

"The Clash have become a messy conglomerate of present day Don Quixotes. So credible, so concerned, and so in control of their output, that from behind a mixing desk, they can now tilt at more non-existent windmills than even the Pentagon is aware of."

'Melody Maker's' Patrick Humpries was a little kinder:

"The odd highlights are lost in a welter of reggae/dub overkill ... (the LP) suggests – in its bewildering aimlessness – that the band are floundering, uncertain of their direction,"

while Robbi Millar, in *'Sounds',* was still more charitable when she wrote:

"It's tempting to think that they've merely hung their album on a cause, albeit a good one, without thinking about the consequences."

But it was Nick Kent in *'New Musical Express'* who most accurately verbalised the feelings of the majority of the media about 'Sandinista' when he wrote:

"This record is strong testimony that The Clash have – temporarily at least – lost a grip on their bearings and find themselves parked in a cul-de-sac," and went on "Some absurdly sycophantic reviews from across the Atlantic have very probably blinkered them to their own strengths and shortcomings."

The price of the triple set was a bargain – that was at least one item on which everyone could agree, although whether the claims made at the time about the group's enormous financial sacrifices were true – it was claimed that in order for the set to be priced at £5.99 (or less, in certain shops), the group would have to sell 200,000 copies in Britain before they would earn any royalties – it's difficult to discover. Another problem which certainly didn't assist the record's chances of immediate huge sales was that John Lennon was murdered in New York just as 'Sandinista' was released, and the vast quantities of money spent around the world on Beatles and Lennon products served to put any other record very much in the shade.

Added to these potential pitfalls was the well-known record industry adage that most double albums would make excellent single LPs if the dross and self-indulgence were removed – the same is presumably even more true of a triple album ...

Almost inevitably, few people admitted to enjoying all of 'Sandinista', whose title came up during the recording of the album, as Joe told Paul Du Noyer:

"I was singing this song, 'Washington Bullets', and I didn't have 'Sandinista' written down, and I got to a verse about Nicaragua. I just came out with it, I just shouted it out. And when I got out of the vocal booth, Mick said 'That's the name of the album' and I started thinking about it. I only found out about the Sandinistas through a friend of mine in San Francisco sending me literature – I'd never read it in the daily rag – so we figured we might as well use that space, it'd be printed everywhere. You could have some hip phrase, but it's more use like this."

In fact, 'Washington Bullets' was a prime target for the critics – one called the track "South American marimba-scraping" and it was also noted that Joe "seems preoccupied with solemnly naming hero after hero" (the song's lyrics mention Allende, Victor Jara, Castro and the Dalai Lama). But the main target was

the diversity of musical direction which permeated the three records – the first side of the first LP is a good example of the many different forms of music on display which, perhaps not unreasonably, few found completely to their taste. 'The Magnificent Seven' is a 'rap' song by Joe in the style of The Sugarhill Gang, 'Hitsville UK' is a duet sung by Mick Jones and Ellen Foley, over a backing track in the Tamla-Motown style, on the subject of the rise of independent record labels. The third track, 'Junco Partner', is an old blues which Joe claimed to have learned from a budget album and which he used to play during his time in The 101-ers, and it's followed by 'Ivan Meets G.I. Joe', which portrays the showdown between East and West as though it had occurred in New York's notorious 'exclusive discotheque', Studio 54. 'The Leader' tells the story of a disgraced politician as it might have appeared in the Sunday popular newspapers, and the final track on the first side, 'Something About England', makes a point about immigrants being blamed for the deterioration of British life, and incorporates a brass band. As Nick Kent noted, the track could be viewed as

"so preposterous and precious, it sounds like a Jethro Tull song."

Evidently, there was almost too much variety in 'Sandinista' for most people to be able to digest, and even though it can hardly come as a surprise to discover that in many cases rock critics have insufficient time to listen to records they are reviewing as much as perhaps they should, it would appear that only the low price prevented 'Sandinista' from becoming a comparative failure, at least initially. Later on, when the album had been properly digested, many people arrived at a point where 'Sandinista' was re-evaluated and discovered to be far more worthy of praise than early reviews had suggested. Perhaps surprisingly, it was listed in the LP charts in America for several weeks longer than in Britain, but this may have been largely due to the American infatuation with The Clash which had begun with 'Train In Vain' a year before. Otherwise, it is difficult to understand how the majority of Americans reacted to the inclusion of two tracks ('Broadway', a Joe Strummer lament, which ends with a brief version of 'Guns Of Brixton' and 'Career Opportunities') sung variously by Mickey Gallagher's children or 'Lose This Skin', sung and written by Tymon Dogg, who had apparently first taught Joe to play a chord on guitar, and had also introduced him to busking, or even yet another Mickey Dread track, 'Living In Fame'.

Inevitably, The Clash (represented by Joe Strummer on this occasion) were quizzed about their intentions as regards 'Sandinista' by the music press. Talking about the varied musical styles displayed by the album, Joe told Paul Du Noyer in *'New Musical Express'*:

"We're not afraid to play around. What we're doing now is experimenting. But I'll only put on a record if it's worth listening to. I hate music that's so concerned with being new that it forgets to have any soul – we experiment, but with those limitation: it's gotta be worth listening to."

And on the political views expressed in several of the songs, Joe told Du Noyer:

"We're getting a lot more political in our old age. As I get older, my politics are clarifying themselves, becoming more pointed, more potent . . . My politics are definitely left of centre, yet I believe in self-determination. I don't believe in Soviet Russia at all, because there's hardly any choice – you've still got a ruling class riding around in big cars."

Talking to Pete Silverton of *'Sounds'* on the same day as he had appeared in court to face charges following the SPG bust of a few months before (Joe was fined £100 for possession of home grown marijuana), Strummer admitted that there was a "a lot of American influence" on the album, but denied suggestions of self-indulgence, saying:

"I won't take any of that – we're taking the rap for our indulgence by not taking any royalties on the first 200,000. We're not saddling the consumer."

When it was mentioned that he seemed to have become more willing to promote 'Sandinista' than some of The Clash's earlier LPs, Joe displayed a grasp of the realities of life, which had perhaps been partially obscured by idealism in the early days, when he said:

"I think you've gotta get out in the market place. It's all too easy to be like the big scene poet and stumble off snivelling into your rat hole – in fact, it's a temptation. We've gotta sell 200,000 for a start. You've gotta be proud of what you do and go out and sell it. Selling ain't nothing to be ashamed of. We employ people and we've gotta pay their wages week after week."

This somewhat more 'mature' view of things was emphasised when Silverton mentioned that one of the criticisms of Sandinista' was that The Clash had become 'professional'. Joe responded:

"I should bloody hope so. If you do something for a while and you don't get better at it, you've got to be stupid. It might seem like we're trying to prove something but we were just trying to do what we couldn't do before. We're always trying to play what we haven't been able to play before. I've taken an oath to really try and learn how to play guitar – so far, it's always been all six strings or none of them."

Perhaps this new desire for self-improvement was helped along by Joe's involvement in the release, in early 1981, of an album by The 101'ers, his pre-Clash band. He told Pete Silverton:

"There's a live tape of us trying to impress a Van Der Graaf Generator audience, and the dog came onstage. I'd been working the audience as hard as I could, and I couldn't get nothing out of them, and then Trouble, the dog, wandered onstage and they all went bananas. And I gave up. The tape's really good

— *fast number banging into another fast number. No messing about, no sloppiness.*"

Of course, neither Joe nor drummer Richard Dudanski (later with Public Image Ltd.) nor lead guitarist Clive Timperley, who went on to join The Passions, would probably claim that they were at the height of their musical abilities during The 101-ers' days ... Nevertheless, when the album, titled 'Elgin Avenue Breakdown' was released, it showed that the band were very much in the 'pub rock' mainstream, much of their material being in the rhythm & blues mould which character-ised the music to be heard in London pubs just before punk rock took over. 'Junco Partner' was included,

providing an instant comparison with the 'Sandinista' version, although inevitably the version by The 101-ers, which was recorded on a cassette off the mixing desk at a concert at the Roundhouse, was somewhat rough technically. Obviously, the attack which Strummer's vocals with The Clash demonstrated wasn't some-thing he picked up when he left The 101-ers, but on the other hand, the LP includes a version of a song with the title of 'Surf City' (but not the familiar Jan & Dean number) which sounds not unlike Crosby, Stills & Nash, something which Joe probably wasn't too keen on. However, that was obviously the exception, as overall, 'Elgin Avenue Breakdown' is a raw and exciting album of some historical significance.

ELLEN'S NEW IMAGE

Unfortunately, the reaction to the LP which Mick Jones produced for Ellen Foley was somewhat less enthusiastic – Ellen had first come to public notice as a result of duetting with Meat Loaf on his multi-million selling LP, 'Bat Out Of Hell', and her début solo album had been largely in a similar vein. When she met Mick Jones and began a romantic relationship with him, it was a natural progression for Mick to produce her second LP, 'Spirit Of St. Louis', which he did. This also credits as backing players all four members of The Clash, as well as several of Ian Dury's Blockheads and Tymon Dogg. Dogg in fact also wrote three of the songs on the album, while Joe and Mick collaborated on another half dozen – it was almost a Clash album, in everything but Ellen's singing and the fact that she was the featured artist. The duet vocals of Ellen and Mick, first unveiled on 'Sandinista's' 'Hitsville UK', were utilised on several tracks, but it would appear that 'Spirit Of St. Louis' was neither a commercial nor critical success, featuring for just two weeks near the foot of the British LP charts, and not even touching the U.S. Top 200 LP chart.

The other 1981 LP in which Mick (plus Topper and indeed Ellen) was involved, Ian Hunter's 'Short Back 'n' Sides', co-produced by Mick Ronson and Mick Jones, and with backing assistance from Mick Jones and his associates, certainly fared better commercially in America, although its showing in Britain was no better than Ellen's. However, it must have been a thrill for Jones to work with one of his early idols – Mott The Hoople, the band led by Hunter in the early 1970s, was one of Jones' favourite groups At least, Hunter's album was not subjected to the kind of critical disapproval which greeted Foley's – one critic likened 'Spirit Of St. Louis' to Moira Anderson singing songs written by Abba!

At least one member of The Clash was having more success with outside work – Topper Headon had bought a timpani some time before, but found that it had been stolen from the New Symphony Orchestra and returned it to them. To show their gratitude, the Orchestra invited Topper to play with them as 'guest percussionist' at a concert held at the Royal Albert Hall on February 1st, 1981. Topper reportedly enjoyed himself immensely, appearing during the Orchestra's performance of Tchaikovsky's '1812 Overture'. Apparently, the concert was a sell out,

"the first gig they'd sold out for a long time, because of all the publicity,"

according to Topper, although he was somewhat upset that he was being "patronised" by the media, who were interested in a "punk rocker goes classical" story, which, of course, was not the point …

'Hitsville UK' was released as a single in Britain, but enjoyed very limited success, spending only four weeks in the UK chart and not even getting as high as the Top 50. In America it failed to even touch the charts when it was released as a single in February, 1981, although this was probably of far less concern to everyone involved because the 'Sandinista' package was crashing into the American LP charts at that time, eventually spending nine weeks there with a highest position of 35. The conquest of the colonies was becoming more and more complete as each album was released.

Back in England, The Clash had announced that they would be touring before long, probably encouraged by CBS, who no doubt expected that the group would conform to the usual pattern of touring behind the release of a new LP. In fact, 'Sandinista' was only in the LP charts for a month and a half, and never showed in the Top 20, so perhaps a tour at this point would have been an advantage to both the group and the company. However, The Clash were anxious to play in what they saw as 'alternative' venues – Kosmo Vinyl even suggested, with an element of seriousness, that anyone with any ideas along the line of wharfs, docks and empty aircraft hangars should write to 'New Musical Express' – but as no suitable places came to mind, the tour was called off. Joe Strummer told one journalist:

"We're not prepared to slog around the country – we've done enough of that already. The band will decide how to go about touring, not the music business."

So England had to manage without them for a while.

BERNIE'S BACK

The major news of the early part of 1981 was that, in a move which surprised almost everyone, The Clash were reunited with their original manager, Bernie Rhodes, in March. Perhaps Joe gave a clue when he told Paul Du Noyer in 'NME' during an interview concerning Sandinista':

"We fell out with Bernie, he lost control of us, and it's a pity we fell out with him because we made a good team. But he got really funny when The Clash started to happen, and we wouldn't see him from week to week. If he wanted to communicate, he'd just send a minion – inferring he was too busy elsewhere to deal with us. We got the phrase 'Complete Control' off Bernie. I remember him going – he'd obviously been talking to Malcolm (McLaren) and was trying to be the master puppeteer – 'Look, I want COMPLETE CONTROL', and we were laughing at him."

In the meantime, since splitting with Rhodes, the group had made substantial progress in many areas, but still obviously felt vulnerable in business terms. Perhaps Rhodes was the only person they knew whom they felt they could trust, but ever since, The Clash have moved smoothly forward, with fewer and fewer unnecessary diversions, which would indicate that their choice was inspired. It was also rather urgent that there should be someone strong representing The Clash, as abandoning the projected British tour had resulted in numerous unsavoury and incorrect rumours indicating that the group were on the verge of splitting up. Soon after reclaiming the reins, Bernie announced that the end of April would see an extensive European tour followed by yet another American tour, while the next British tour would be in the autumn.

Meanwhile, Joe Strummer decided to run unofficially in the first London marathon, and despite the lack of fibre and fitness which it is generally assumed rock stars suffered from, Joe acquitted himself reasonably. The manner in which Topper Headon made the news was less positive – he was given a conditional discharge for a year after admitting possessing heroin and cocaine. Also, a new single was released, featuring two versions of the opening track of 'Sandinista', 'The Magnificent Seven'. One side was the familiar track, but the other was a remixed version of the song with added Latin American percussion (among other things) titled 'The Magnificent Dance', which sounded like a restrained dub – the remix was done by Puerto Rican producer, Pepe Unidos, but the record wasn't a huge commercial success, although it briefly reached the British Top 40, but once again made no American chart impression.

Around this time, a feature was published in the New York magazine, 'Musician Player and Listener' in which Joe and another British guitarist, Robert Fripp,, perhaps most famous as leader of King Crimson but also notable for having played with David Bowie, interviewed each other. The results showed that despite their widely different personalities, the two had remarkably similar ideals, and even if there were few subjects on which both agreed, one unlikely topic about which they shared the same view was the Swedish pop group, Abba, whom both admitted to liking. The European tour was predictably a great success, with the opening gigs in Spain the group's first for nearly a year, but the highlight was in Lyons, France, where they attracted a crowd of more than eight thousand people. Possibly the support showed by European fans was what motivated Bernie Rhodes to suggest that the group should spend an extended period, perhaps nine months, away from Britain.

The American tour was something else again – once more, no doubt because of the low price of 'Sandinista' – from which they could expect a long wait until they could make a profit, Epic Records refused to finance a complete tour, and it became clear that some sort of compromise would be necessary for The Clash's American fans to be able to see them playing live. Following their appearance at the New York Palladium in 1980, the group had refused to play in the city unless they could perform in a venue which they considered suitable, an unseated dance hall, so their scheduled seven night season at Bond's a night club/discotheque near Times Square, seemed a fair solution to the problems, as it would not involve long and tedious journeys in between gigs. It was also announced that no free press tickets would be available, although a limited number would be on sale at half price for a few selected writers.

CHAOS IN NEW YORK

Although everything seemed to have been well planned, when the season began, chaos ensued. $10 tickets were selling for five times their face value – hardly what The Clash had intended – but a much greater problem ensued when the New York Fire Department announced after the first night's show that for the rest of the season, they were going to enforce the legal capacity of Bond's, which was set at 1750 people. This limit is supposed to ensure that in the case of a fire, everyone in the audience ought to be able to get out of the club in safety – on the first night, the Department said, the audience amounted to nearly four thousand people, and even though people who were there subsequently said that it didn't seem painfully crowded, the Department ruled that if there had been a fire, only half the people would have been able to escape easily. After the second night's show, the New York City Building Department acquired a court order to close the club, although there were whispers that this was not unconnected with a night club war being waged in New York at the time, which had previously resulted in the closure of several clubs. When that was announced, the crowd on the pavement outside went berserk and had to be cleared by mounted police.

Eventually, a compromise was reached when the City's Building Commissioner (apparently following a great deal of personal pressure exerted by his children, who were Clash fans) agreed that The Clash could complete their season (by now extended to sixteen consecutive nights, which would allow everyone who had bought a ticket to attend a show, but forced projected gigs at Bond's by both Gary Glitter and The Stranglers to be postponed) if security and fire escapes were improved.

The concerts themselves were not exactly trouble-free – American girl singer Pearl Harbour, who was there as disc jockey, was apparently given a difficult time, but this was nothing compared to the intense disapproval which greeted the various support acts. Both Funkapolitan and British girl group The Slits found things difficult, but the worst roasting was apparently given to local rap king Grandmaster Flash and The Furious Five. Nevertheless, The Clash played to a very positive response, taking the stage to the recorded strains of 'For A Few Dollars More', the theme music to Clint Eastwood's spaghetti western, and also previewing what would be their next single, 'This Is Radio Clash', to general approval.

In various interviews conducted during both the European and American tours, the members of The Clash demonstrated that some of their views about life were starting to change – Mick Jones told Paolo Hewitt:

"I've found out something quite important about people in England. It seemed that when they were turning against us, it was because they were annoyed with us, and the reason they're annoyed with us is because we can't make it. If you're stuck in Sunderland or Newcastle and you've been following The Clash for a few years, and you see The Clash banging their heads against this brick wall ... If people are a bit more open minded in terms of receiving us, then it's better, because that's when the exchange of ideas and communications comes where we can actually capture people and perhaps make people understand. We play much better if people are digging it than if they're fighting us. There's no sense in that, it's stupid."

This was obviously a matter which Mick had been thinking about a lot, because he told Mick Farren during the New York stint:

"I don't worry about making it, I worry about not making it. If I don't make it, then all the kids who are watching can say to themselves: 'Well, shit, they didn't make it, they didn't get out. What hope is there for us to make it?' If we make it, then those kids know that they've got a chance too."

Joe, on the other hand, had obviously spent his spare moments thinking about politics – as he told Alan Lewis for 'Sounds',

"I believe in the Socialist way. I don't know any more than that. I don't know any system to save the world, but I believe that socialism at least has more humanity in it."

At the same time, Joe denied that he and the rest of the group were so committed to the cause that they perused socialist propaganda –

"You've really got us wrong, we're not like that at all. We're political in the sense that our words don't deal in love all the time, but if you think we read 'Socialist Worker', you must be out of your mind. I can't read that journalism because it's so slanted and biased that it's worthless."

Other events which occurred in New York included The Clash auditioning for a part in a film due to be made by Martin Scorsese and starring Robert De Niro, and Topper announcing that he would be producing some records for another of the groups who had opened for The Clash at Bond's, The Bush Tetras. It was also noted by one critic that Headon seemed to be "out of his brain most of the time" an unhappy preview of a state of affairs which would once more threaten the future of the group in the months to come.

ON THE ROAD AGAIN

However, there were other concerns in the immediate future – at long last, a British tour was announced, although the choice of venues did not appear to please everyone, as of the thirteen dates, seven were to be held at the Lyceum Ballroom in London's Strand, while the provincial dates were limited to just six. This tour was to commence at the start of October, immediately after a week of gigs at the Mogador theatre in Paris – for some reason, the Mogador was due for demolition as soon as The Clash's season was over. During their week in Paris, the group were interviewed by Paul Rambali of 'New Musical Express', who took the opportunity to confront the group with some of the criticisms that 'NME' writers, who had been among the most ardent Clash supporters from the start, were voicing. Mick Jones, when asked why he behaved like a superstar, admitted that there were "traditional elements" to his work, adding:

"A good guitar solo in the right place, a little bit of tension added to the show – there's nothing wrong with having respect for the stage, because you're also out there entertaining."

Jones also confessed that he had been disappointed with the reaction to the album he produced for Ellen Foley, and when asked in an oblique manner where The Clash had been during the celebrated Toxteth riots in Liverpool during the summer, defended his own absence (which the group's early fans conceivably considered unforgivable) by saying:

"I don't think I'd make such a great rioter . . . I don't even know if I agree with them. Destroying your own places, especially if the government ain't going to give you another one, seems really double dumb. I do my thing, and it's a creative thing – that's how I feel I contribute to that. And if my absence is conspicuous on these occasions, then I say don't look to me in the first place. I'm not the street fighting man. I've still got a belief in the power of reason."

Rambali's article also revealed a number of hitherto little known facts about Mick and particularly Joe – Mick had apparently attended Hammersmith (later renamed Chelsea) Art School, where he studied towards 'A' Levels for one year and went to evening classes to achieve sufficient qualifications to be accepted for a foundation course, while Joe's early years had been far

more exotic – born in Ankara, Turkey (his father was a British diplomat), and lived in Cyprus, Mexico City and West Germany before being sent to boarding school, where he got three 'O' Levels, in English, History and Art. After that it was London's Central School Of Art, and after that The 101'ers and The Clash. Joe also took the time to defend himself again over the question of The Clash's altered image and look when he said:

"We could do it two ways – we could write the same songs, perform the same way on stage, but we could all wear C&A outfits. Either you go up there for people to look at you or you stay at fucking home! When I see people going on stage in any old shit, I think 'You mugs! Do you think people enjoy standing down there? They want to see something.' It's such a hideous thing anyway – you might as well make the effort."

The concerts, both in Paris and London, were widely criticised in the press, despite what most writers saw as an increase in professionalism. With New York graffiti artist Futura 2000 actually painting the stage set while the group were performing, transforming it, as one reviewer noted, into something resembling a border post between two countries, the general consensus seemed to be as described by the 'New Musical Express' reviewer, who described the material on both 'London Calling' and 'Sandinista' as "piffle", also noting:

"There's Strummer trying not to be Strummer, but all the same emitting that absurd screech about five times during the course of every song. There's Jones flopping about like a Pete Townshend puppet and playing some of the worst guitar the Lyceum has probably ever witnessed, and there's Simonon looking more like that oaf in 'Rude Boy' every year."

What seemed to be annoying longtime fans was suggested by one writer who commented:

"The Clash's music has lost a lot of its abrasive power – the short sharp volatile statement has been replaced by the long, meandering and convoluted,"

although a few critics, notably in 'Melody Maker', saw things rather differently, one calling the group

"disciplined, controlled and working with an almighty zest, showing that they are back

with a fresh impetus."

Despite the many reservations, it was clear that most of the original Clash fans were very pleased to see their favourite group back on a British stage.

Plans were being made for the next album, and at this time a rather unexpected bonus occurred in terms of a cover version of a Clash song by an artist who, although not very well known, was almost as far from being a 'punk' or 'New Waver' as is possible. Tom Gribbin, a country/rock singer from Florida, decided to record his own version of Paul Simonon's 'Guns Of Brixton'. Although Gribbin admitted that he didn't know very much about the situation in Brixton, he rationalised his interest in the song by telling Richard Wootton of *'Melody Maker':*

"The song made a lot of sense to me in context with the Confederate soldiers who returned home after the American Civil War and found themselves dispossessed – men like Jesse James and Cole Younger, who had to turn to crime for survival."

Although The Clash obviously didn't need to resort to breaking the law in order to survive, comparisons with the James Gang were probably right up their street – however, Gribbin's 'Guns Of Brixton' was not a huge commercial success. Rather less gratifying was a seemingly misconceived attempt by The Clash to raise money for redundant steel workers in the town of Corby in the South Midlands – they provided a 1970 model Cadillac car, which was supposedly worth £3,000, as the first prize in a raffle whose proceeds would go towards a welfare fund for the jobless workers. While the gesture seemed very helpful, the winner of the car told the press that not only was the car not driveable, but a garage had told him that it was worth nothing other than as scrap metal, for which he had received an offer of £100. As he had already spent rather more than that on transporting the car to his home, he was substantially out of pocket. In fairness, it should be noted that the car had been acquired by The Clash as a result of a bet made by Radio One disc jockey Anne Nightingale, and probably neither the group nor Ms. Nightingale were aware of the car's poor condition, so that their donating it to the steel workers' cause was certainly not intended to produce the effect it did. Still, it was an unfortunate incident . . .

77

CLASH ON THE AIRWAVES

By the time news of the Cadillac controversy was published, The Clash were in New York, working on their new LP back at Electric Ladyland studios. Almost simultaneously, 'This Is Radio Clash' was released as both a seven inch and twelve inch single in Britain and purely as a twelve inch EP in the U.S.A., but it was not a great success by Clash standards, only managing just over a month in the UK charts and not featuring at all in America. Quite obviously, the group were not too concerned, as they were much more involved in making a success of their new LP. This time it was to be simply one record, rather than the two or three which had seemed to be becoming the rule, although Tymon Dogg, who had featured on 'Sandinista', was on hand again, and so were other friends like Ellen Foley, legendary beat poet Allen Ginsberg, Texan country/rock star Joe Ely, with whom they had become friendly in America, and Futura 2000. With Futura, the group also recorded a track on which they appeared simply as a backing band, 'The Adventures of Futura 2000', although there was some doubt as to whether they would be allowed to be credited on the record if and when it was released. Also on the subject of 'outside' projects, it transpired that Mick Jones had produced the first LP by Theatre Of Hate, 'Westworld'. The group, which was led by singer/guitarist Kirk Brandon, splintered at the end of 1982 when Brandon left to form a new band, Spear Of Destiny, but 'Westworld' seems to have been their finest moment, and briefly reached the Top 20 of the British LP charts. Additionally, the Clash as a whole were also involved in an all star compilation album, 'Life In The European Theatre', the proceeds of which were used to benefit disarmament and anti-nuclear organisations. The LP kicks off with 'London Calling', and among the other acts who contributed their services to this cause were The Jam, The Beat, Peter Gabriel, XTC, The Specials, The Undertones and Madness.

As soon as the new LP was completed, the group travelled to the Far East for tours of Australia and Japan, with Paul Simonon's girl friend, American singer Pearl Harbour, along for the ride. The nine Japanese gigs saw The Clash being granted what is apparently a very rare privilege in that the audience were allowed to stand up – perhaps as a gesture of thanks, 'London's Burning' was specially performed as

'Tokyo's Burning' ... It was also announced during the course of the tour that the next British tour would take place in the late spring of 1982, to coincide with the release of the new album.

Even during spare time on the Australian leg of the Far East tour, the group were in the studio adding refinements to the new LP, which they had produced by themselves, although later on they would make the inspired decision to allow veteran British producer Glyn Johns to remix their work. Johns had previously worked with virtually every major British group during the 1960's, including The Beatles, The Rolling Stones, The Who, The Kinks and The Small Faces, as well as with a number of notable American acts like Steve Miller and The Eagles.

The enormous improvement in the quality and clarity of the recorded sound of The Clash came as a welcome bonus, if not a relief, to many critics who had been supporting the band for five years now, but were beginning to wonder whether all their predictions about world domination and success on a major scale were ever going to come true. It was probably with great gratitude that X. Moore in 'NME' called 'Combat Rock' "easily the best Clash album since 'Give 'Em Enough Rope'" and Dave McCullough in 'Sounds' called it "Strummer's best work since 'The Clash', in fact, his only work since 'The Clash'." For once, there could be no complaints about inferior or messy sound

Glyn Johns' remix had seen to that – although surely many of the original Clash fans might have squirmed when they saw that McCullough continued by saying: "It's closer to Fleetwood Mac's 'Rumours' (which it is very like) than 'The Clash'."

Not everyone liked the new direction – Mark Cooper in 'Record Mirror' rather uncharitably stated: "The Clash can no longer punch their way out of a paper bag" and the 'Melody Maker' review even complained about the look of the album, which it called "especially unpleasant". In fact, 'Combat Rock' (whose original title was supposedly to have been 'Rat Patrol From Fort Bragg', which might have made the record seem as obscure as 'Sandinista' to early Clash fans) was a very normal single LP in a single sleeve which also contained a large colour poster of the band. At first hearing the twelve tracks sounded far smoother than anything done previously by The Clash, but of course

this was somewhat deceptive, as most of the songs contained a message of some significance. 'Know Your Rights', for instance, has Joe intoning "Murder is a crime unless it was done by a policeman or an aristocrat", and as the LP's title implies, much of it reflects the group's views on politics, the problems of inner city life, and war.

'Atom Tan', for example, is a scenario relating to life after a nuclear holocaust, and Paul Simonon's 'Red Angel Dragnet' is about New York's 'Guardian Angels', whose aim is to make the city safe for ordinary people after dark, particularly the subways, but there are also surprises, like the involvement of 1950s beat poet Allen Ginsberg, who recites a poem in 'Ghetto Defendant' which is heard in the gaps in Joe's singing, or 'Over-powered By Funk', which features vocals by

Futura 2000. Ellen Foley can be heard on 'Inoculated City' and Tymon Dogg on 'Death Is A Star', and strings and horns are also in evidence – but what was perhaps most unexpected, particularly since the first single from the LP, 'Know Your Rights', received a distinctly cool welcome from record buyers, charting for a mere three weeks in Britain and not even reaching the Top 40, was the amazing feat of the album in crashing straight into the British LP chart at number two – it didn't make the magic top position, but quite obviously was destined to become their biggest seller ever. The latest CBS biography of the band indicates that this success "astounded" them, but perhaps it was an indication that The Clash were now playing (and winning) the game of commercial success using old established rules.

JOE DOES A RUNNER

However, there was a major cloud in the sky which diluted the joy which The Clash should have been feeling at this triumphant time – at the end of April, 1982, just after the release of the 'Know Your Rights' single and just before 'Combat Rock' hit the shops, and perhaps even more crucially, immediately before a twenty date British tour which had been scheduled to help promote the album, Joe Strummer disappeared. After doing an interview with a Scottish newspaper in London, he simply vanished, and although there were a number of reported sightings of Joe and his girl friend in various parts of Britain and Europe, the only report with a ring of truth came from music writer Steve Taylor of 'The Face', who claimed to have shared a compartment with Joe on a boat train to Paris on the day after the interview.

Among cynical record industry veterans there were suggestions that Joe's absence was a carefully plotted move to draw attention to the release of the new LP, but this seemed unlikely as his not being available also meant that the tour would have to be at least partially cancelled, or rescheduled if Joe should reappear. Inevitably, manager Bernard Rhodes was asked for a statement, and was quoted widely as saying:

"Joe Strummer's personal conflict is 'where does the socially concerned rock artist stand in the bubblegum environment of today?' I feel he has probably gone away for a serious rethink."

By the middle of May, when 'Combat Rock' appeared, Joe was still missing, nearly all the tour dates had to be cancelled, and The Clash were in disarray, although one positive item was that Joe had contacted relatives to say that he was alive and well, even if he didn't say where he was. Maybe it was lucky that 'Combat Rock' was doing so well – if Joe had vanished at any other time, it might easily have spelt the end of The Clash.

Towards the end of May, Joe was found, apparently as a result of Kosmo Vinyl getting involved in some 'detective work', in Paris, and persuaded to rejoin the group just in time for a live appearance at a festival in Holland. Joe's return, after a month's absence, must have been an enormous relief to everyone involved with The Clash, and also to many of their fans, but another blow was on the way – on their return to London after the Dutch gig, Topper Headon announced that he was leaving the group, and when asked why, issued a statement which said that it was **"due to a difference of opinion over the politi-**

cal direction the group will be taking,"

although at the time, this seemed like an exceedingly inadequate answer. There was no question of the group breaking up completely, and it was also announced that on their imminent American tour, guest drummers would be used, and that the British dates which had been cancelled due to Joe's absence would be rescheduled to take place after the completion of the U.S. tour.

Somewhat surprisingly, there were very few interviews with the group to elaborate on all the activity, but one writer who was granted an audience was Charles Shaar Murray of 'New Musical Express'. About Headon's leaving the group, Strummer told Murray:

"It was his decision. I think he felt it's not too easy to be in The Clash, it's not as simple as being in a comfortable, we're-just-entertainers group, and he wanted to do that, just play music."

This was still a little unconvincing, particularly in view of the fact that it had been openly suggested on a number of occasions over the previous months that the drummer seemed to have a drug problem, but Joe's own dramatic disappearance and return were even more important as talking points.

Joe told Murray:

"It was something I wanted to prove to myself, that I was alive. It's very much like being a robot, being in a group. You keep coming along and keep delivering and keep being an entertainer and keep showing up and keep the whole thing going. Rather than go barmy and go mad, I think it's better to do what I did, even for a month. I just got up and went to Paris . . . without even thinking about it. I only intended to stay for a few days, but the more days I stayed, the harder it was to come back because of the more aggro I was causing that I'd have to face there."

Neither Mick Jones nor Paul Simonon seemed very annoyed with Joe, despite the chaos his vanishing had apparently caused, and Simonon noted:

"The fact that he went just cleared the air and made you realise more of where you stood individually as well as to two or three other people. I knew he was coming back."

Another result of the interview with Murray was the

JOE DOES A RUNNER

information that American release of 'Combat Rock' had been delayed as the group wanted the sleeve re-printed omitting the record company propaganda message suggesting that home taping of records was killing music. According to Kosmo Vinyl: "We don't care how many people tape our records," but far more significant was the statistic that 'Sandinista' had very nearly sold the required 200,000 copies in Britain which would mean that The Clash were no longer heavily indebted to CBS.

When 'Combat Rock' did come out in America, it didn't storm the charts in the same way as in Britain, but after entering the Top 200 at number 99 in June, gradually climbed up the chart until it was in the Top 10 by Christmas, and by that time had obviously easily outsold every previous Clash release. The first American single from the album was, perhaps unsurprising-ly in view of its rather militant and outspoken lyrics, not 'Know Your Rights' but 'Should I Stay Or Should I Go', one of the less abrasive songs on the album, which

was sung by Mick Jones and featured some lyrical lines in Spanish, although musically it was reminiscent of The Rolling Stones. As it appeared more or less simultaneously with the album on which it was includ-ed, a highest position of 45 was fairly respectable.

Around the time the single was released, the apparently luckless Topper Headon was in trouble again when he made an appearance in court, accused of stealing a bus stop valued at £30, and also of handling some stolen hi-fi equipment. He was remanded on bail … Meanwhile, the reunited Clash were checking out possible drummers for the Ameri-can tour, and the choice finally fell on their original rhythm ace, Terry Chimes, although it was stressed that the arrangement was, at least initially, only temporary. After leaving The Clash to make way for Topper, Chimes' main work had been with Cowboys International, a band he formed with Ken Lockie, although this was not the most commercially success-ful of enterprises.

RIOTOUS ASSEMBLIES

This being The Clash, the American tour was not exactly the smoothest running affair, although it would be wrong to blame the group for the fireworks thrown from the crowd during the opening gig at Asbury Park, New Jersey, a place made famous by Bruce Springsteen, who titled his first LP after the seedy seaside town. One of the bangers exploded as it hit Joe's knee, and he was rushed to a local hospital and treated for minor burns. But this was trivial compared to the so called riot which erupted at the next gig, in Atlanta, Georgia, where a crowd of people described by the local press as 'neo Nazis', who had apparently aligned themselves with The Clash without the group's knowledge or permission, tried to distribute political literature to members of the departing audience and also began threatening those who wanted nothing to do with them. Inevitably, fights broke out, and fourteen people were arrested by the police and a couple of policemen received minor injuries. At the same time, rumours began to circulate that Topper Headon was about to rejoin the band, apparently started by one of the drummers who auditioned for the job who claimed that he had been turned down for that reason.

After completing the American tour without further mishap, Britain once again looked forward to having their favourite rebels onstage, and an interesting idea was proposed to make the tour more memorable – the group intended to turn every venue into a club (to be known as the Casbah Club, in line with the group's new single, 'Rock The Casbah'), and it was also suggested that if the English football team were to reach the World Cup Final (coinciding with The Clash appearing at Brixton's Fair Deal) that the match would be televised live as a "support act", although it must be said that it seemed most unlikely that the England team would make such notable progress, which in fact was the case. Two other items of interest came up at the start of the British tour: Joe Strummer had a new hair style, a 'Mohican'; while almost equally odd was the information that an American manufacturer of toilet bowl cleaners with the highly appropriate name of Flushco Inc. were sueing The Clash over the song 'Inoculated City' which is included on the 'Combat Rock' LP. Flushco claimed that the song was based on one of their advertising jingles!

Also, Dave McCullough of 'Sounds' returned to Britain after having seen The Clash on tour in Los Angeles, interviewing Joe Strummer, who was obviously feeling that it was once again time for The Clash to be represented in the British music press. As well as several interesting, if less than vital pieces of information, such as that he intended to run more marathons, but would be going into training in future, and that he was actually married:

"I married a non-British (woman) for £150 to buy a guitar. I can't manage to get divorced, though – I can't seem to find my wife, that is, I can't seem to remember her name. That sounds ridiculous, I know, but that name . . . it just won't come back to me. It's like a novel."

Joe came clean about one or two things. About the return of Terry Chimes.

"We had to find a drummer within five days before this tour, and we couldn't think of anybody except Terry. We just went for what he knew, so we're playing the old stuff on this tour. I still kinda like that old material."

After McCullough noted that the old material sounded fresh, Strummer commented:

"I think we're really desperate, really hungry again, because Topper's left and we feel vulnerable again."

And on that topic, Joe apparently confirmed the rumours which were already circulating to the effect that he himself had personally fired the ex-drummer because of his involvement with what was described as 'nasty substances'.

About his disappearance, Strummer said

"I just got up and went! My girlfriend's mother is in jail in France, so I had a personal reason to go there, but I did literally get up and go. I went to shake The Clash up, to shake The Clash fans up, to shake The Clash haters up, and to shake myself up too."

With 'Rock The Casbah' well on its way to restoring The Clash to the British Top 30, from which they had been absent for the best part of two years (since 'The Call Up'), the critics found the group largely revitalised and

back to something like their full potential. Richard Cook in *'NME'* wrote: "The Clash have moved this year as if time is really running out, for them and us. What they have done is familiar enough to most groups facing up to a mid-life menopause: re-examine their beginnings and climb a different path back. The Clash have reinvented their roots ... and have learnt to channel sounds as never before. What the bungling theatre of sorts that now calls itself British punk cannot grasp is this definition. Most of them could learn again from a group they now presumably laugh at; the sound of punk shouldn't be the spluttery sprawl of mud-clogged feedback over Chad Valley drums, it should be this steeled rush, this fluorescent razor's edge!" Mike Nicholls in *'Record Mirror'* was somewhat less poetic, but noted: "Delivery is still exciting, yet a lot more controlled, the almost calculated calmness inevitably

introducing a lot more tension into the playing. That this did not spill over into the audience is some indication of the greater maturity they now encourage and adopt," while *'Melody Maker's'* Adam Sweeting ended his review with: "We were entertained by a rock 'n' roll band which is incapable of slickness (thank God) and has learned to replace bullshit with more songs." The tour was obviously a huge success, to the point where extra dates had to be added in response to enormous demand for tickets – only a month before, Joe Strummer had told *'Sounds'* that The Clash were "struggling" to sell out the British tour!

Not that the group, or at least Joe Strummer, were becoming complacent – as he told *'Record Mirror'*:

"I can't sleep anymore. I'm still awake at 6.30 every morning, and I've been like this for

about six months, since I gave up dope. A joint's as good a sleeper as Valium and I'd been smoking for about ten years. I had to stop. I'm in search of my memory, in search of my dreams. I want to be able to go to sleep and dream and wake up remembering what I've dreamt."

Joe also admitted that he felt that despite their initial beliefs, The Clash would probably be unable to alter any of the things which they had set out to destroy.

"We tried to do something else, we thought there was some truth to be said in music. We were definitely trying to usher in a new age, and it hasn't happened, that's why we're dodos, anachronisms. Perhaps we've been blowing the trumpet where no note is called for, maybe all the western world has to offer is a pretty tune and a few words that don't mean anything. I feel high and dry and beached though I know we're still the best live band and we can still blow anyone offstage."

Perhaps his pessimism was partially lifted when his long-lost wife reappeared, although her quote to *'NME'*;

"I was thinking of settling up, but I've seen his new haircut and heard his recent single. Really, I guess I'm just too embarrassed to admit to what was a grave mistake,"

was hardly designed to make him feel anything but regretful over the whole situation.

THE SUMMER OF '82

One positive aspect of the summer of 1982 for Clash fans was the appearance of 'The Punk Rock Movie', made in 1977 by erstwhile disc jockey Don Letts, who went on to make several proclaimed promotional videos for The Clash, who of course appeared in the film. Letts was due to work on a second film featuring The Clash, 'Clash On Broadway', featuring live clips of the band performing songs like 'Radio Clash' and 'Rock The Casbah'. Patrick Humphries, who saw early extracts of the film, noted: "It looks as though the new film has captured that raw, sublime power of The Clash which 'Rude Boy' comprehensively failed to do."

The rest of the summer of 1982 was strangely quiet for Clash watchers, broken only by the suggestion that Topper Headon was about to join a new band being formed by 'Fast' Eddie Clarke, ex of Motorhead, and Pete Way, ex of UFO, although eventually the alliance did not take place, while it was also suggested that Allen Ginsberg, who had appeared on 'Combat Rock', was scheduled to cut two further tracks with the group.

Then came commercial success on both sides of the Atlantic, as in Britain, a new single, 'Should I Stay Or Should I Go', reached the Top 20, while simultaneously, 'Rock The Casbah' achieved a similar status in the American singles chart. Half The Clash were also spotted performing a brief few songs in New York, where a reunion between four 'survivors' of the 'Anarchy' tour of 1977, in the shape of Mick Jones, Terry Chimes, Johnny Thunders and Steve Jones took place on stage at the Peppermint Lounge. But what must have been the final nail in the coffins of any original Clash fans came with the news that the group had agreed to a booking as support act for The Who at Shea Stadium, the vast arena which had become known throughout the world of popular music as a result of a massive concert there by The Beatles during the 1960s. When the concert took place in October, 1982, one eye witness reported that The Clash sounded just like any other support band, although admitting that they had to battle with heavy rain, the usual poor sound quality which tends to spoil stadium gigs, and the steady flow of aircraft circling the nearby La Guardia airport in New York.

Of somewhat greater significance was The Clash's appearance at the first Jamaica World Music Festival held in Montego Bay in November, where they shared the bill with a number of other world famous names, including Aretha Franklin, The Beach Boys, The Grateful Dead and Gladys Knight, among numerous others. This seemed to have been a happier occasion for the group according to Richard Grabel in 'New Musical Express' who wrote:

"The Clash took their chance and made it mean something,"

while it was also surmised shortly before Christmas that there were possible plans for a first Clash live LP to be released, recorded at the Shea Stadium concert. The year ended with the news that 'Combat Rock' had become the group's first gold album in the United States, and that platinum status was expected imminently.

Apart from the announcement of a projected European tour to include some British dates, plus the reissue of their classic first album at a semi-budget price, the early part of 1983 saw little Clash action. The earlier suggestion that The Clash would be appearing in a new Martin Scorsese film starring Robert De Niro was largely confirmed – the film, 'King Of Comedy', besides starring De Niro and Jerry Lewis, would also include rôles for Joe Strummer, Mick Jones, Ellen Foley and Pearl Harbour, who had apparently got married to Paul Simonon some time before.

After several more weeks of silence, it was announced that Terry Chimes had once again left The Clash. He told the press:

"We all had a great time, but now it's time to get back to my own plans, which got neglected for the last nine months," and Joe Strummer added: "Terry put up with a lot of pressure on the British and American tours, but I only saw him throw a tantrum once, which is truly remarkable. He snapped after six hours in a mini-bus with everyone singing 'Terry and Bernie/Live together in perfect harmony' to the tune of 'Ebony and Ivory'. I thank him for the laughs as well as the drums."

Chimes was not immediately replaced, and it wasn't until the end of March that any mention was made of a new drummer, and even then, Derek Goddard, an ex-member of The Raincoats, was not confirmed as a permanent member of the group, although he had apparently worked with The Clash.

Something rather odd also seemed to happen to 'King Of Comedy' – despite closing credits acknowledging the presence of Mick and Joe plus Ellen Foley and Pearl Harbour, only Kosmo Vinyl and Joe's girlfriend, Gabrielle, were visible in the film when it was

premièred in New York, although the group apparently still did provide some music for the film's soundtrack.

More than a year after the release of 'Combat Rock' in Britain, there was still no concrete news of a further album, and the media were forced to resort to either non-musical activities or Clash-related gossip to keep the group in the public eye. For example, it was reported that Jimmy Carter, ex-president of the United States, and his wife, had altered their listening habits, and instead of an endless musical diet of American bands like The Allman Brothers, were listening to up and coming British acts like The Clash and The Jam, having been introduced to the 'modern world' by their children. Concurrently, it was also reported that the group had been booked for a large sum (variously half a million or a million dollars), to play at the second 'Us' Festival, to be held near Los Angeles in May – the festival supposedly represented "the marriage of rock and technology".

PLATINUM ALBUM

Meanwhile, 'Combat Rock' had achieved platinum status in America, a most significant achievement and acknowledgement that The Clash were now part of the rock establishment whether they liked it or not – it was probably no coincidence that Kosmo Vinyl was quoted as saying:

"When a band as politically direct as The Clash gets through to over a million people, you know there's some hope left in the world."

Back in Britain, the Clash-connected news was mixed – Joe Strummer again ran in the London Marathon, but this time as an official entrant sponsored by 'The Sun' a daily newspaper whose political views he seemed most unlikely to share. However, in the absence of any politically preferable sponsors, it was certainly a smart move to accept help from someone, as competing in such an exhausting event as a marathon requires substantial back up support. In the event, Joe successfully completed the course in just over four and a half hours (not bad – it's over twenty-six miles) which was ten minutes better than his previous personal best.

The one off single The Clash had made with Futura 2000 was also released, on the Celluloid label in America, and on Charly Records in Britain, under the title 'The Escapades Of Futura 2000', but most reviewers seemed to regard it as nothing too special. Somewhat sadder news, especially for Topper Headon, was that Pete Farndon, an ex-member of The Pretenders, had been found dead. After the planned band with Pete Way and Eddie Clarke had fallen through, Headon and Farndon had been playing together with a view to jointly forming a new group.

As 1983 meandered onwards, with unemployment still rising, and little sign of the end of the recession, The Clash were in a healthier position, at least in terms of status within the rock world, than ever before. Of course, there were still problems – a new LP was due, yet it wasn't until the end of May that a permanent replacement for Topper Headon was announced, after auditions which reportedly involved more than 300 applicants for the job. The final choice was Peter Howard, a virtually unknown 23 year old from the city of Bath, who had previously worked with a somewhat less celebrated CBS recording group, Cold Fish.

An even bigger delay looked likely after it was announced in late August, completely out of the blue, that Mick Jones had been fired by Joe and Paul. One possible reason for this momentous decision was suggested by an unnamed acquaintance of the band

– after hearing that The Clash intended to perform at the 1983 Notting Hill Carnival, the acquaintance was informed by a most reliable source that the projected appearance had been cancelled since Mick wasn't talking to the rest of the group.

In statements released by CBS at the beginning of September, Strummer and Simonon stated:

"It is felt that Mick Jones should leave the group. He has drifted apart from the original idea of The Clash. In future, it will allow us to get on with the job The Clash set out to do from the beginning."

Jones, in retaliation, said the official press statement was untrue. He made it clear there was no discussion with Strummer and Simonon prior to his sacking, he had not drifted apart from the original idea of The Clash, and in future he would be carrying on with the same dedication as in the beginning.

This came in addition to Mick's romance with Ellen Foley petering out shortly before, and occurred at a most inopportune moment. For the first time, vast numbers of Clash fans on both sides of the Atlantic were eagerly awaiting a new record, after the great success of 'Combat Rock'.

Shortly before the end of 1983, after several months silence, Clash spokesman Kosmo Vinyl announced that the group would be touring in Britain early in the New Year although no clue was given as to a potential replacement for Jones. In the meantime Janie Jones, immortalised on The Clash's first album, had resumed her recording career with a single entitled "House Of The Ju Ju Queen" with considerable help from Joe Strummer.

A few days into 1984 the new line-up of The Clash was announced. In addition to Joe (now apparently abandoning his guitar to become lead vocalist), Paul and Peter Howard, two new guitarists had been recruited: Vince White, from Finsbury Park, and Nick Sheppard from Bristol, previously a member of early British punk band The Cortinas. This was to be the new Clash line-up although they had no immediate plans to record.

The one slightly jarring feature of the start of 1984 was that Mick Jones and Topper Headon, who could possibly have as much claim to the name The Clash, were said to be working together on an album for release in the spring of 1984. In characteristic style matters were shrouded in uncertainty. Nothing involving them has ever been straightforward and probably never will be.

DISCOGRAPHY

U.K. SINGLES

White Riot//1977
CBS 5058 Released 18/3/77

Remote Control/London's Burning
CBS 5293 Released 13/5/77

Complete Control/The City Of The Dead
CBS 5664 Released 23/9/77

Clash City Rockers/Jail Guitar Doors
CBS 5834 Released 17/2/78

(White Man) In Hammersmith Palais/The Prisoner
CBS 6383 Released 16/6/78

Tommy Gun/One Two Crush On You
CBS 6788 Released 24/11/78

English Civil War/Pressure Drop
CBS 7082 Released 23/2/79

The "Cost Of Living" EP
CBS 7324 Released 11/5/79

London Calling/Armagideon Time
CBS 8087 Released 7/12/79 (also released on 12in.)

Bankrobber/Rockers Galore . . . UK Tour
CBS 8323 Released 26/7/80

The Call Up/Stop The World
CBS 9339 Released 21/11/80

Hitsville UK/Radio One
CBS 9480 Released 16/1/81

The Magnificent Seven/The Magnificent Dance
CBS A1133 Released 10/4/81 (also released on 12in.)

This Is Radio Clash/Radio Clash
CBS A1797 Released 4/12/81 (also released on 12in.)

Know Your Rights/First Night Back In London
CBS A2309 Released 23/4/82

Rock The Casbah/Long Time Jerk
CBS A2479 Released 18/6/82 (also released on 12in.)

Should I Stay Or Should I Go/Straight To Hell
CBS A2646 Released 17/9/82

U.K. ALBUMS

The Clash
CBS 82000 Released 8/4/77

Give 'Em Enough Rope
CBS 82431 Released 10/11/78

London Calling
CBS CLASH 3 Released 14/12/79

Sandinista
CBS FSLN 1 Released 12/12/80

Combat Rock
CBS FMLN 2 Released 14/5/82

U.S. SINGLES

I Fought The Law/(White Man) In Hammersmith Palais
Epic 9-50738 Released 1979

Train In Vain (Stand By Me)/London Calling
Epic 9-50851 Released 1980

Hitsville UK/Police On My Back
Epic 19-51013 Released 1981

The Call Up (12in. EP)
Epic 48-02036 Released 1981

This Is Radio Clash (12in. EP)
Epic 49-02662 Released 1981

Should I Stay Or Should I Go/various B-sides
Epic various numbers released 1982

Rock The Casbah/Long Time Jerk
Epic 14-03245 Released 1982 (Also on 12in.)

U.S. ALBUMS

Give 'Em Enough Rope
Epic JE35543 Released 1978

The Clash
Epic JE36060 Released 1979

London Calling
Epic E2 36328 Released 1979

Black Market Clash
Epic 4E3 6846 Released 1980

Sandinista
Epic E3X37037 Released 1980

Combat Rock
Epic FE37689